DATE

MW01122293

THOMAS HOBBES AND THE POLITICS OF NATURAL PHILOSOPHY

Continuum Studies in British Philosophy:
Series Editor: James Fieser, University of Tennessee at Martin

Duncan Richter, *Wittgenstein at his Word*
Wilfrid E. Rumble, *Doing Austin Justice*
María J. Frápolli (ed.), *F.P. Ramsey: Critical Reassessments*
William R. Eaton, *Boyle on Fire*
David Berman, *Berkeley and Irish Philosophy*
Colin Tyler, *Radical Philosophy*
Stephen Lalor, *Matthew Tindal, Freethinker*
Michael K. Potter, *Bertrand Russell's Ethics*
Angela M. Coventry, *Hume's Theory of Causation*
Colin Heydt, *Rethinking Mill's Ethics*
Stephen J. Finn, *Thomas Hobbes and The Politics of Natural Philosophy*
John R. Fitzpatrick, *John Stuart Mill's Political Philosophy*
J. Mark Lazenby, *The Early Wittgenstein on Religion*
Dennis Desroches, *Francis Bacon and the Limits of Scientific Knowledge*
Megan Laverty, *Iris Murdoch's Ethics*
William C. Davis, *Thomas Reid's Ethics*
John H. Sceski, *Popper, Objectivity and the Growth of Knowledge*
Talia Mae Bettcher, *Berkeley's Philosophy of Spirit*
Eric Brandon, *The Coherence of Hobbes's Leviathan*
Patricia Sheridan, *Locke's Moral Theory*
J. Jeremy Wisnewski, *Wittgenstein and Ethical Inquiry*
Rosalind Carey, *Russell and Wittgenstein on the Nature of Judgement*
Michael Taylor, *The Philosophy of Herbert Spencer*
James E. Crimmins, *Jeremy Bentham's Final Years*
James G. Buickerood, *John Locke on Imagination and the Passions*

THOMAS HOBBES AND THE POLITICS OF NATURAL PHILOSOPHY

STEPHEN J. FINN

continuum

Continuum
The Tower Building
11 York Road
London SE1 7NX

80 Maiden Lane
Suite 704
New York
NY 10010

British Library Cataloguing-in-Publication Data
A catalogue record for this book is available from the British Library.

ISBN: HB: 0-8264-8642-8

Typeset by BookEns Ltd, Royston, Herts.
Printed and bound in Great Britain by MPG Books Ltd, Bodmin, Cornwall

For Joan

Contents

Abbreviations for Hobbes's Works

B	*Behemoth*
Ci	*De Cive*
Co	*De Corpore*
D	*A Dialogue between a Philosopher and a Student of the Common Laws of England*
El	*Elements of Law*
EW	*The English Works of Thomas Hobbes of Malmesbury*
L	*Leviathan*
OL	*Thomas Hobbes Malmesburiensis opera philosophica quae latine scripsit omnia*
PPG	*Principia et Problemata aliquot Geometrica*
SL	*Six Lessons to the Savilian Professors of the Mathematics*
ST	'A Short Tract on First Principles'
T	*Eight Books of the Peloponnesian War written by Thucydides the Son of Olorus, interpreted with Faith and Diligence immediately out of the Greek by Thomas Hobbes*

References to Hobbes's works are cited in the text with the abbreviations listed above. References to *Ci*, *Co*, *El* and *L* are to chapter and page number. References to *EW* are to volume and page number. References to *B*, D, *OL*, *PPG*, *SL*, ST and T are to page numbers.

1
Background and Goals

1.0 Introduction

In 1642, Thomas Hobbes presented to the world a little treatise on political philosophy (*De Cive*) that contained, at least in his opinion, the first *science of politics*. Hobbes believed his political philosophy achieved a scientific status because it was modelled on geometry, which is the 'onely science that it hath pleased God hitherto to bestow on mankind' (*L* 4.105). An earlier version of his science of politics, i.e., the *Elements of Law*, had been privately circulating in manuscript form in 1640. Readers of this book would discover a political philosophy grounded on the 'rules and infallibility of reason', both of which provide the 'true and only foundation of such [a] science' (*El* Epistle xv–i). Eleven years later, in 1651, Hobbes published his masterpiece that would put him in contention for being one of the pre-eminent political philosophers in English history. In *Leviathan, or the Matter, Forme, and Power of a Commonwealth Ecclesiasticall and Civill*, which contains the most developed version of his political philosophy, Hobbes reaffirmed the scientific nature of his views. This work, like its earlier counterparts, presented a 'true doctrine of the laws of nature', which is the heart of Hobbes's 'science of virtue and vice' (*L* 15.216). For the first time in human history, Hobbes believed, a science was available that would provide indisputable answers to political problems, and thereby promote peace and stability in the commonwealth.

If Hobbes's philosophy offered genuine solutions to persistent political problems, it could not have come at a better time in

English history. In 1642, civil war erupted in England after many years in which, as Hobbes said, the nation was 'boiling hot with questions concerning the rights of dominion and the obedience due from subjects, the true forerunners of an approaching war' (*Ci* Preface 103). Political turmoil, although percolating for many years, had become especially acute in the two decades prior to the outbreak of war. In 1625, Charles I inherited not only his father's crown, but also his desire to run the country without interference from Parliament, a desire that faced numerous obstacles. One such obstacle was Parliament's control of the primary sources of taxation. When the King needed substantial funds, he was often forced to turn to Parliament for assistance. As might be expected, the Members of Parliament were unwilling to offer such assistance since it required them to perform the unpopular task of taxing their constituents. Financial disputes between King and Parliament marked the 1620s, as is evidenced by the fact that Charles used forced loans on numerous occasions. In 1628, for example, the King relied on forced loans to support his war efforts against Spain and France when subsidies were not granted by Parliament. Such financial problems contributed to political tensions that culminated in a civil war and, eventually, in the beheading of the King. The execution of Charles in 1649, however, did not put an end to the political unrest. A continual shifting of political power caused civil disorder until the Restoration of Charles II in 1660. After completing *Leviathan*, which was published in 1651, Hobbes hoped that his work would 'fall into the hands of a Sovereign' who might 'by the Publique teaching of it, convert this truth of speculation, into the Utility of Practice' (*L* 31.408).

Hobbes's political philosophy, as the name suggests, reveals his practical interest in *politics* and his theoretical interest in *philosophy*. These two interests dominated his life. His long-standing concern with political matters is clearly evidenced in the history of his written work. In 1628, at the age of 40, Hobbes published the first work of his extended literary career, a translation of Thucydides'

History of the Peloponnesian Wars. According to his autobiographical writings, the goal of publishing this translation was to point out how 'foolish democracy is, and how much wiser one man is than an assembly' (*OL* xxxviii). The translation was followed by the writing of three versions of his political philosophy, concluding with *Leviathan*. In 1668, Hobbes wrote *Behemoth*, which presents an historical account of the causes of the English Civil War. One year later, Hobbes composed a dialogue on the nature of law called *A Dialogue between a Philosopher and a Student of the Common Laws of England*.

While a number of works attest to Hobbes's political interests, his writings in natural philosophy and his active involvement with contemporary scientists manifest his interest in scientific and abstract philosophical questions. In his biography of Hobbes, John Aubrey recounts his subject's first experience with geometry.

> He was ... 40 years old before he looked on geometry; which happened accidentally. Being in a gentleman's library ..., Euclid's Elements lay open, and 'twas the 47 *Ellibri* I. He read the proposition. 'By G–,' sayd he (he would now and then sweare, by way of emphasis), 'this is impossible!' So he reads the demonstration of it, which referred him back to such a proposition; which proposition he read. That referred him back to another, which he also read. *Et sic deinceps*, that at last was demonstrably convinced of the truth. This made him in love with geometry.[1]

Whether the details of Aubrey's story are historically accurate does not need to be confirmed here. What is important is that Hobbes's discovery of geometry prompted him towards natural philosophy. According to some scholars, Hobbes's first work in natural philosophy was composed early in the 1630s, a work commonly referred to as 'A Short Tract on First Principles'.[2] In this tract, Hobbes lays out a number of mechanistic principles from which conclusions about optics, metaphysics and human motion are derived. In 1642, Hobbes wrote a criticism of Thomas White's *De Mundo*. As a Catholic theologian, White attempted in this text to refute Galileo. In 1644, Hobbes's 'Tractatus Opticus' was published in Paris by Marin Mersenne. Shortly thereafter, in 1646, Hobbes became a mathematical instructor to the Prince of Wales, who would later become Charles II. Hobbes's most comprehensive work in natural philosophy, *De Corpore*, was published in 1655. In this work, Hobbes provides an extended discussion of philosophical methodology, geometry and physics. Hobbes's *Six Lessons to the Savilian Professors of the Mathematics*, wherein he responds to criticisms of his work by eminent mathematicians, was published in 1656. Hobbes criticized the methodology of Boyle in *Dialogus Physicus de Natura Aerae*, published in 1661.

Hobbes's practical concern with political affairs and his theoretical interest in natural philosophy are united in his political philosophy. In this book I am concerned with the relationship between these two components of Hobbes's philosophy. According to what I call the 'traditional interpretation of influence', which shall be more fully discussed in Chapter 2, Hobbes's natural philosophy, and especially his fascination with geometry, plays an influential role in the formation and evolution of his political ideas. I will attempt to reverse the traditional direction of influence by pointing out ways in which Hobbes's political ideas influence his natural philosophy. To elaborate further upon the particular nature of my project, I will situate it within the context of Hobbes scholarship in Section 1.1. In Section 1.2, I will provide a brief outline of the remaining chapters.

1.1 Scholarly Background

In this section, I relate this investigation to four areas of scholarly research on Hobbes. First, I discuss two interpretive approaches, one of which considers Hobbes primarily as a theoretical philosopher and the other of which considers him primarily as a political advocate. Second, I present an overview of the scholarly attempt at solving the 'problem of unity', which is the problem of relating the different branches of Hobbes's philosophy to each other. Since I am concerned with the relationship between Hobbes's political philosophy and his natural philosophy, the problem of unity needs to be discussed. Third, I discuss the notion of a 'political influence' and how this notion is employed in Hobbes scholarship.

1.1.a Interpretive Approach

In *The Obsession of Thomas Hobbes*, Jules Steinberg is highly critical of what he sees as the tendency of Hobbes scholars to treat him as a 'disinterested philosopher', rather than as a 'traditional political philosopher'.[3] According to Steinberg, the majority of scholars interpret Hobbes as a disinterested philosopher, that is, as a thinker who first and foremost advances philosophical arguments about theoretical matters. In this case, although Hobbes explicitly states that his political philosophy offers a scientific solution for the disorders of his time, his science is not specifically designed for seventeenth century England. Instead, Hobbes's philosophical arguments are supposed to transcend the particular historical situation from which they emerged. Howard Warrender, for example, takes this approach when he attempts to 'discover the logical structure of his [Hobbes's] argument'.[4] According to Warrender, Hobbes is a philosopher who is 'clearly interested in logical and not historical analysis'.[5] Although Warrender recognizes the presence of 'historical examples' in Hobbes's texts, these examples 'carried little significance for Hobbes, who saw the problem of sovereign and subject as a problem of logical principle and not of practice'.[6] Hobbes's political philosophy, in other words, is more about theory than practice. John Plamenatz, as well, is an adherent of this approach. In his *Man and Society*, Plamenatz claims that 'to understand Hobbes we need not know what his purpose was in writing *Leviathan* or how he felt about the rival claims of Royalists and Parliamentarians'.[7] Plamenatz undertakes a 'close study of his argument' without 'looking at the condition of England or at political controversies of the day'.[8] In a similar manner, Anthony de Crespigny and Kenneth Minogue argue that the '*Leviathan* is a complicated argument from which nothing at all follows directly or logically about what, in terms of the quarrels of seventeenth century England, should be supported'.[9] The basic idea behind this interpretive approach, or what I call the 'philosophical approach', is that Hobbes thinks of himself as primarily engaged in a philosophical and scientific activity, rather than in the advocacy of a specific political agenda.

One should note that in extreme cases of the philosophical approach an investigation into Hobbes's intentions plays virtually no role in the interpretation. The goal in such cases is to analyse, evaluate and improve upon Hobbes's arguments for the sake of the arguments themselves. Accordingly, determining Hobbes's own intentions is inconsequential to the principal duty of constructing a viable philosophical argument. It is not important to determine, in other words, whether Hobbes is primarily a philosopher or a political pamphleteer. Instead, as philosophers, our job is to stick to the arguments themselves. Gregory Kavka, for example, follows such a path in his *Hobbesian Moral and Political Theory*. 'The ultimate goal', Kavka says of his book, is 'to explicate and defend a plausible system of moral and political hypotheses suggested and inspired by Hobbes'.[10] Thus, Kavka claims, 'while not Hobbes's own theory, the theory set forth in this book is surely Hobbesian'.[11] Kavka is more interested in critiquing and improving upon Hobbes's arguments than in understanding the intentions behind them.[12]

According to Steinberg, advocates of the philosophical approach are motivated by the desire to keep Hobbes's philosophical arguments free from the damning charge of being 'ideological'.

[T]his is the fundamental point of most contemporary Hobbes

scholarship: the denial that Hobbes was writing about anything associated with the English Civil War. However, this denial is justified by a widely-held conviction that to interpret Hobbes as a political philosopher writing about the English Civil War is to disparage these writings by suggesting that they are ideological rather than philosophical.[13]

Steinberg claims such scholars hold fast to the view that 'philosophers do not advocate, prescribe, recommend, or justify in their political writings'.[14] Steinberg is obviously quite hostile to the philosophical approach. It is, in his opinion, 'absurd and misleading',[15] 'ludicrous in the extreme',[16] 'absurdly wrong'[17] and a 'mis-conceived dead end'.[18] He contends the philosophical approach is based upon the fundamental and mistaken assumption that 'political philosophers never write in isolation from actual historical events and political circumstances'.[19]

Steinberg's alternative to the philosophical approach is to treat Hobbes as a 'traditional political philosopher' and to interpret his political philosophy in light of his political intentions:

> Let me restate what I am suggesting when I claim that Hobbes wrote as a traditional political philosopher. This means that Hobbes was directly engaged in the practical business of advocacy or justification, that Hobbes wrote with a 'practical purpose in mind,' that this latter consideration was provoked by Hobbes's reaction to the political crisis that led to the English Civil War, and that Hobbes was writing to condemn certain ideas and behavior and to support alternative ideas and behavior. From this perspective, it is absurd to claim that Hobbes wrote with any kind of 'disinterested attitude.'[20]

I will refer to Steinberg's interpretive strategy as the 'political approach'. According to the 'political approach', one interprets Hobbes primarily as a political advocate, and secondarily, if at all, as an abstract philosophical thinker.

The choice between the political and philosophical approaches is often related to the decision to include historical factors in one's interpretation. Adherents of the political approach frequently interpret Hobbes within an historical context, taking into consideration such things as the social and political circumstances of seventeenth-century England, events in Hobbes's personal and private life, and other such factors. The philosophical approach, on the other hand, usually focuses on the arguments themselves and often overlooks historical information.

Steinberg gives the impression that a philosophical approach necessarily excludes historical analysis. In this case, however, Steinberg falls prey to what Quentin Skinner calls a 'widespread tendency to insist that the interpretation of Hobbes's texts and the study of their historical contexts are alternative undertakings'.[21] Despite this tendency, a number of the philosophical interpreters do emphasize the importance of historical factors. John Watkins, for example, claims historical information is necessary for an accurate philosophical interpretation of Hobbes:

> Although this book is an essay in logical reconstruction its approach will not be unhistorical. It is, after all, *Hobbes's* ideas whose organization we shall investigate; and in trying to establish what a man's ideas are, one should use any available information about his problems, his intentions, his political and intellectual situation, about his contemporaries and their readings of him, and so on.[22]

Although Watkins appeals to history, his orienting principle is that Hobbes's philosophy, including his political philosophy, is grounded on a 'number of *purely philosophical* ideas'.[23] In this case, then, historical information is employed in a 'logical reconstruction' of Hobbes's philosophy, in keeping with the philosophical approach.

Quentin Skinner and A. P. Martinich are two scholars who

believe historical information is necessary for an adequate interpretation of Hobbes. According to Skinner, 'there are many
elements in Hobbes's science of politics that we have no hope of
explicating unless we pay attention to the circumstances out of
which they arose'.[24] Martinich similarly claims that 'interpreting or
understanding what a person meant equally involves attributing
certain beliefs and intentions to the speaker, and the basis for
attributing these beliefs and intentions depends to a great extent on
contextual features'.[25] In taking an historical approach to Hobbes,
Martinich is 'not suggesting that a non-historical approach has no
value'.[26] Instead, he is 'suggesting that a purely non-historical
approach is virtually impossible' since 'every scholar has some
historical knowledge of a philosopher's context and uses it in his or
her interpretation'.[27] For these philosophers, it is necessary to use
historical information to understand Hobbes's arguments.

The difference between the philosophical and the political
approach really boils down to a distinction in emphasis.[28] The
'philosophical approach' interprets Hobbes primarily as a philosopher who is first and foremost concerned with theoretical questions
and secondarily concerned, if at all, with the practical implications
of his theory for his own time. The 'political approach', on the
other hand, views Hobbes primarily as an advocate of a specific
political agenda and secondarily as a theoretical and abstract thinker.

In this work, I use both a philosophical and a political approach.
Insofar as I employ a philosophical approach, I examine a number of
inconsistencies that arise within Hobbes's natural philosophy. In so
doing, I focus on arguments in Hobbes's texts without reference to
historical considerations. In contrast to Skinner and Martinich, I am
inclined to accept the validity of an unhistorical approach, at least in
the case where one's goal is to evaluate the internal structure of
Hobbes's philosophy. Of course, as Martinich points out, a
completely unhistorical approach is 'virtually impossible'.[29] An
interpreter of Hobbes's texts, for example, must be aware of the
difference between seventeenth-century English and contemporary

English. Putting aside such general contextual knowledge, however, an examination of Hobbes's arguments for their philosophical consistency without reference to historical information is a legitimate enterprise. Insofar as I discuss the internal consistency of Hobbes's philosophical ideas, then, I utilize the philosophical approach. In addition to pointing out inconsistencies in Hobbes's philosophy, however, I attempt to *explain* why they arise. It is in this endeavour that I employ a political approach. Hobbes, I believe, is definitely not a disinterested philosopher concerned primarily with abstract and theoretical issues. The political upheavals of seventeenth-century England, as he himself attests, are a cause of his philosophical interest in political matters.

1.1.b The Problem of Unity

One of the most prevalent questions in Hobbes scholarship is whether the various parts of his philosophy form a unified system. Hobbes divides philosophy into natural philosophy, moral philosophy and civil philosophy. In *De Cive*, Hobbes reveals his intention of presenting his entire philosophy in three stages, each of which focuses on a different type of body: natural, human and civil. 'In the first', he says, 'I would have treated of *body* and its general properties; in the second of *man* and his special faculties and affections; in the third of *civil government* and the duties of subjects' (*Ci* Preface.102–3). This neat tripartite division is clouded by the fact that human beings are both natural bodies and citizens of commonwealths, thus Hobbes's moral philosophy seems to be subsumed under both natural philosophy and civil philosophy. The three branches of philosophy, in other words, are ultimately reducible to two. In *Leviathan*, Hobbes suggests such a reduction when he divides philosophy into natural philosophy and civil or political philosophy (*L* 9.148). In this case, moral philosophy or 'ethiques', which studies the 'consequences from the Passions of men', is found under natural philosophy. In *De Corpore*, on the other hand, Hobbes specifically divides civil philosophy into 'ethics' and 'politics' (*Co* 1.11). This problem of classifying Hobbes's moral philosophy in relation to natural and civil philosophy is merely a symptom of the larger problem of relating all of the parts of his philosophy together.

Before I address this larger problem, I want to clarify my use of certain terms. In keeping with scholarship, when I refer to Hobbes's 'natural philosophy', I mean the content of *De Corpore*, which includes his views on geometry and physics, and his account of human sensation and voluntary motion. Hobbes's 'moral philosophy' will refer to that part of his natural philosophy concerned with humans insofar as they are natural bodies. By Hobbes's 'civil' or 'political' philosophy, I mean the part of his philosophy dealing with the relationship between humans outside of political institutions and with the construction, maintenance and dissolution of the commonwealth.

With regard to how the parts of Hobbes's philosophy are related to each other, scholars generally fall into one of two camps. On the one hand, the 'systematic' interpreters claim that the branches of Hobbes's philosophy are connected to each other in some fundamental way.[30] On the other hand, the 'non-systematic' interpreters view the branches of Hobbes's philosophy as independent sciences that are not related to each other in any important ways.[31]

According to the systematic interpretation, Hobbes's philosophy is viewed as a chain argument that deduces the conclusions of political philosophy from the premises of natural philosophy, via the principles of human nature. According to this interpretation, Hobbes employs the resolutive-compositive method used by Galileo and the philosophers of the Paduan School. In the words of David Gauthier: 'We resolve, or as Hobbes often prefers to say, analyse a whole – a watch, or a commonwealth – into its constituent parts, discovering the relations among the parts, which then enable us to recompose or synthesize the whole.'[32] This method works by resolving the commonwealth into its parts (i.e., human bodies), and resolving these parts into their parts (i.e., passions and desires), and then resolving these into their parts (i.e., the motions of natural bodies). After such resolution is accomplished, the compositive method is used to reconstruct the commonwealth beginning with the fundamental principles of natural science.

The systematic interpretation is widespread in Hobbes scholarship. C. B. Macpherson claims Hobbes follows the Galilean method 'by resolving political society into the motions of its parts – individual human beings – and resolving their motions in turn into imagined or hypothetical or simple forces which, compounded, could be shown to explain them'.[33] 'In accordance with the synthetic or geometrical mode of proceeding,' another systematic interpreter claims, 'one would begin with the laws of physics in general, from them deduce the passions, the causes of behavior of individual men, and from the passions deduce the laws of social and political life.'[34] Gary Herbert, in his *Thomas Hobbes: The Unity of Scientific and Moral Wisdom*, offers the most recent attempt at revealing the systematic nature of Hobbes's philosophy. The stated intention of Herbert's book is to 'restore Hobbes's thought to its more traditional philosophical location' by 'taking seriously his clearly stated intention to produce a "system" of philosophy, grounded upon physics, working through an egoistic account of human nature to a realistic account of civil association'.[35] Systematic interpreters claim, to put it briefly, that Hobbes intends to deduce the conclusions of political philosophy from the principles of natural philosophy.[36]

John Watkins adheres to a variant of the systematic interpretation when he contends that Hobbes's philosophy constitutes a system, but denies that 'Hobbes deduced his psychological principles from physical principles'.[37] Instead, Watkins says the ideas expressed in Hobbes's natural philosophy 'collectively imply' many conclusions in civil and political philosophy.[38] The point for Watkins is that Hobbes does not actually present his system in the form of a scientific demonstration. Instead, Hobbes only provides the raw materials for one. This point is best explained through Watkins' example wherein he asks us to imagine that Hobbes, on different occasions and with different intentions in mind, wrote the following statements in his journal: 'all kings are men', 'all men are mortal'. From these two statements, one can conclude that all kings are mortal, even if Hobbes does not draw this conclusion himself. For Watkins, the principles of Hobbes's natural philosophy imply the conclusions of his moral and civil philosophy in this fashion.[39]

Hobbes provides evidence for the systematic interpretation in those cases where he says the principles of each science are related to each other as links in a deductive chain. In *De Corpore*, for example, Hobbes claims the principles of political philosophy are based on psychological principles: 'the principles of politics consist in the knowledge of the motions of the mind' (*Co* 6.74). Knowledge of mental phenomena, in turn, seems to depend on physics since 'mental motions' have their 'causes in sense and imagination, which are the subject of physical contemplation' (*Co* 6.73). The principles of politics, in other words, are discovered by an inquiry into mental motions that, in turn, requires a physical investigation into the faculties of sense and imagination. Natural philosophy, according to this interpretation, provides the basis for an understanding of human nature that, in turn, provides the foundation for political philosophy.

In contrast to the systematic interpreters, advocates of the 'non-systematic' interpretation believe the different branches of Hobbes's philosophy are independent sciences that have no substantial connection to each other. Evidence for this interpretation is found in Hobbes's claim that the principles of political philosophy are empirically based and not derived from natural philosophy. In *De Cive*, Hobbes informs the reader that the exigencies of the civil war led him to publish his political philosophy before his natural philosophy. Although the order of presentation was reversed, Hobbes says, it has no effect on the truth of his political philosophy:

'Therefore it happens, that what was last in order [i.e., political philosophy], is yet come forth first in time. And the rather, because I saw that, grounded on its own principles sufficiently known by experience, it would not stand in need of the former' (*Ci*, Preface 103). Leo Strauss refers to the above passage in his defence of the non-systematic interpretation:

> Political philosophy is independent of natural science because its principles are not borrowed from natural science, are not, indeed, borrowed from any science, but are provided by experience, by the experience which every one has of himself, or, to put it more accurately, are discovered by the efforts of self-knowledge and self-examination of every one.[40]

Thomas Sorell, another advocate of the non-systematic interpretation, claims that 'Hobbes's scientific political philosophy is independent of his physics' because its first principles are known by experience.[41] If the principles of political philosophy are empirical, then it is not necessary to derive them from the science of physics. Thus, according to the non-systematic interpreters, Hobbes's political philosophy stands independently of his natural philosophy.

The non-systematic interpretation is buttressed by the fact that the systematic interpretation is mired by three serious philosophical difficulties. In the first case, it is difficult to deduce psychological conclusions from premises in natural philosophy. Bernard Gert, who is highly critical of any attempt at such a deduction, is quick to reveal the problems associated with this task. Regarding the relationship between mechanism and egoism, Gert claims that 'psychological egoism cannot be validly deduced from any version of Hobbes's mechanical account of human behavior'.[42] Gert's position is grounded on the convictions that Hobbes's psychology is concerned with motives and that a mechanistic view of nature cannot include the concepts of motives. According to Gert, 'the fact that psychological egoism is a theory about human motives is sufficient to make it impossible for it to be derived from any mechanical theory, including Hobbes's'.[43] Psychological principles, however, are the necessary link from natural to political philosophy. In the second case, the systematic interpreters must deal with the problem of deriving normative conclusions from factual premises. As many philosophers have pointed out since Hume, it is not possible to derive an 'ought' from an 'is'. The fact that Hobbes's view of human nature is untenable and could not therefore serve as a foundation for his civil philosophy provides a further criticism of the systematic interpretation. In the words of F. S. McNeilly, if Hobbes's civil philosophy 'presupposes the truth of such doubtful – at least disputable – views' then 'his political conclusions must themselves be more doubtful than if they had no such presuppositions'.[44]

In relation to the problem of unity, I will draw on insights from both the systematic and the non-systematic interpretations. First, I accept the fundamental insight of the systematic interpreters that Hobbes's natural philosophy and his political philosophy are intricately related. Yet, whereas most scholars reveal the influence of the former on the latter, I will argue that the influence frequently moves in the opposite direction. Second, I accept the important insight of the non-systematic interpreters that Hobbes's political philosophy does not follow as the final link in a long deductive chain. If it is the case that Hobbes's political ideas influence his natural philosophy, as I will maintain, the former must be independent, to some degree, of the latter.

1.1.c The Political Influence

Although scholars recognize the problem with the relationship of the various branches of Hobbes's philosophy, the notion that one branch may *influence* another is not often explicitly discussed. When scholars do speak of this, whether explicitly or implicitly, they usually assert that Hobbes's natural philosophy influences or structures his political philosophy. Take, for example, the following claim by Watkins.

> Hobbes's method *determined* the shape of his civil philosophy – required it to start by stating what men's condition would be were there no civil authority over them ... And it also *dictated* Hobbes's quasi-democratic account of the origin of political authority. It also *determined* the sort of prescriptive purpose his civil philosophy should have, the kind of imperatives it should yield.[45]

In this passage, Watkins claims that Hobbes's method 'dictates', 'determines', and forces 'requirements' on certain aspects of his civil philosophy. Watkins also claims the 'main thesis' of his book is to show that Hobbes's 'philosophical ideas collectively imply enough of his political theory to provide a drastic solution for the political problems'.[46] The impression given by Watkins is that Hobbes is a disinterested philosopher who lays down a number of strictly philosophical ideas about method, the natural world and human nature, and then deduces political conclusions on the basis of these strictly philosophical ideas. Certainly, Hobbes's own emphasis on the scientific nature of his political philosophy encourages such a reading and, therefore, Watkins' position is understandable.

Leo Strauss, long before Watkins expressed his view, criticized the view that the 'characteristic contents of Hobbes's political philosophy' is 'determined by and, as it were, implied by the method'.[47] Strauss endorses G. C. Robertson's claim that Hobbes's political philosophy had 'its main lines fixed when he [i.e., Hobbes] was still a mere observer of men, and not yet a mechanical philosopher'.[48] More recently, William Lynch similarly argued that Hobbes's political agenda was established prior to his explorations in natural philosophy. Unlike Strauss, however, Lynch claims that traditional interpreters overlook the manner in which Hobbes's political agenda influences his natural philosophy. In 'Politics in Hobbes's Mechanics: The Social as Enabling', Lynch 'aims to unravel one significant direction of influence in the formation of Hobbes's mature philosophy, that of Hobbes's political agenda on his approach to mechanical questions'.[49] Lynch bucks the trend in Hobbes scholarship that denies or disregards any such connection.

> [C]ontrary to the conclusion of most observers, Hobbes's political philosophy is not rooted simply in his natural philosophy. But rather than reversing the connection (an option generally ignored in the literature) or denying any connection, I will show that a pre-existing political *agenda* influenced the position that Hobbes would take in mechanical issues by enabling him to develop a fruitful approach against the background of available approaches.[50]

The notion that Hobbes's political agenda *enables* his science, as we shall see, plays an important and influential role in the goals of the present work. It is therefore beneficial to elaborate upon Lynch's position at this point.

In his article on the enabling role of Hobbes's politics, Lynch takes issue not only with the systematic interpreters, but also with advocates of the 'holistic sociology of knowledge thesis'. In Hobbes scholarship, this thesis is advocated by Steven Shapin and Simon Shapiro in *Leviathan and the Air-Pump*.[51] The 'aim of the historical sociology of knowledge', Lynch claims, is to 'demonstrate the thorough interpenetration of seemingly disparate areas of intellectual and social life, without untangling specific directions of influence'.[52] According to this thesis, the web of political, social and scientific issues are so intertwined that it becomes virtually impossible to reveal unidirectional causal influences. In Lynch's opinion, Shapin and Shapiro's thesis is valid insofar as it emphasizes the connectedness of political and scientific issues. It runs into problems, however, when it places emphasis on the historically contingent nature of Hobbes's views and then attempts to use counterfactual statements to express such contingency.[53] Lynch claims that one must appeal to specific unidirectional causes in order to use counterfactuals in an historical or explanatory account. For example, the following counterfactual claim of Shapin and Shapiro states the notion that different social circumstances would have caused a different reception of Hobbes's scientific views: 'Given other circumstances bearing upon the philosophical community, Hobbes's views might well have received a different reception.'[54] If one strictly adheres to the holistic thesis, it is not legitimate to make such a remark since it does not allow for unidirectional causal claims.

Lynch implies that counterfactual questions play an important role when trying to determine the influence of Hobbes's political agenda on his natural philosophy. So, for example, one might ask whether Hobbes's scientific and philosophical views would have been the same had he possessed a different political agenda. To answer such a question, Lynch proposes the following approach:

> The solution to this impasse, I suggest, is to begin to unravel specific chains of causal influence that bear relevance to the counterfactual questions that concern us, without making further unwarranted claims of overall unidirectional causation, clear separability of different aspects of thought, or the irrelevance of other counterfactual questions highlighting different causal connections.[55]

To determine whether Hobbes's political agenda influences his scientific views, according to Lynch, one should appeal to specific unidirectional causal claims. For if we say that Hobbes's scientific views would have been different, this implies that his political agenda does have a causal influence on his scientific investigations.

In his article, Lynch is concerned with tracing out one specific line of influence in Hobbes's philosophy, viz., the influence of

'Hobbes's political *agenda* on his approach to mechanical questions'.[56] In revealing this influence, Lynch says he is not simply reducing scientific investigation to the forces of political interests.[57] Instead, he asserts that political and social issues *enable* scientific research by opening up new avenues of research or critique:

[O]ne must show how certain specific, historically contingent circumstances influenced scientific development not merely by eliminating certain options but by enabling certain fruitful approaches to arise that would not otherwise have been formulated. The epistemic is not reduced to the social; rather, specific social circumstances influence scientific practice (itself constitutively social) in an epistemically fruitful manner.[58]

To say Hobbes's political agenda *enables* specific philosophical views is not to say the agenda *determines* them. According to Lynch, a number of philosophical positions may provide the same theoretical support for Hobbes's political agenda. For this reason, Lynch speaks of the causal influence in terms of *underdetermination*. 'The precise form of political influence', Lynch claims, 'is underdetermined in the same way that data underdetermines theory.'[59] Lynch suggests that we look at Hobbes's political agenda as a heuristic device that a 'bounded rational agent could use to impose order on disparate fields of inquiry'.[60] According to this interpretation, Hobbes's political agenda encourages him to adopt, develop and use scientific theories in novel ways.

The notion that social circumstances enable scientific research is the starting point for Lynch's investigation into specific counterfactual claims regarding the relationship between Hobbes's politics and his natural philosophy.

I will show that a pre-existing political agenda influenced the position that Hobbes would take in mechanical issues by enabling him to develop a fruitful approach against the background of

available approaches ... Counterfactually, we may claim that
were it not for prevailing political issues and Hobbes's approach
to these issues, certain epistemic failings of contemporary work
would have escaped observation – hence an example of politics
enabling science.[61]

To say that Hobbes's political agenda *influences* his natural
philosophy, according to Lynch, is to say that Hobbes's politics
enables his science by opening up new avenues of research.

I will continue the project begun by Lynch insofar as it reveals the
manner in which Hobbes's political ideas *influence* or *enable* his
natural philosophy. Although Lynch's ideas inform my investigation, there are important ways in which it will extend beyond his
project. In the first case, while Lynch is specifically concerned with
Hobbes's *political agenda* and with his mechanistic view of nature, I
am concerned with his *political ideas* and with other aspects of his
natural philosophy, e.g., his view of truth and his nominalism.
Under the heading of 'political ideas', I include both his 'political
agenda' and his 'political philosophy'. By 'political agenda', I refer to
the specific goals, if any, Hobbes was hoping to achieve in
presenting his political philosophy to his contemporaries. Some
examples of these goals include, but are not limited to, the
following: to establish a state of peace in England, to defend the
sovereign power of King Charles I, to criticize the doctrines of
religious leaders, and to attack the ideas of common law
practitioners. In each case, the aim is directly related to the political
arena of seventeenth-century England. Hobbes's 'political philosophy', on the other hand, refers to his theoretical ideas concerning
the commonwealth. Such ideas include, but are not limited to, the
following: political absolutism, the superiority of monarchy, and the
necessity of a coercive power for civil order. Hobbes's 'natural
philosophy', by contrast, is guided by 'scientific' or 'strictly
philosophical' aims. Such aims include, but are not limited to, the
following: to define the nature of truth, to advocate a particular

philosophical method, to discover the causes of human behaviour, to discover the causes of physical phenomena, and to argue against the existence of Aristotelian species or forms. My project, then, is of a wider scope than Lynch's since it extends beyond Hobbes's mechanism and into his natural philosophy as a whole.

In the second case, unlike Lynch, I argue that Hobbes's political ideas influence him to accept *specific* philosophical positions, i.e., the conventional view of truth and nominalism. While Lynch points out ways in which Hobbes's politics underdetermine his natural philosophy, I make the stronger claim that the political ideas encourage Hobbes to advocate specific philosophical ideas.

In the third case, while Lynch and I both reveal paths of influence, I also attempt to explain inconsistencies in Hobbes's natural philosophy by appealing to his political ideas. As such, this work has an explanatory function that is absent in Lynch's project. For the most part, then, when I refer to the *influence* of Hobbes's political ideas, I refer to their *enabling* power, as Lynch describes it. In some cases, however, I use *political influence* in a stronger sense to mean not only that Hobbes's politics enables his science in an undetermined manner, but that it plays an influential role in his acceptance of *specific* philosophical positions.

My project, and Lynch's, are part of a much wider debate in the 'sociology of knowledge'. The most general question in this debate is: How should one explain scientific belief and theory? The participants in the debate answer in a variety of ways, depending on their different views on the role of 'epistemic' and 'non-epistemic' factors in the explanation of scientific rationality. Epistemic factors are those factors employed by the scientist to explain the rationality of the scientific belief or theory involved. These factors serve, in other words, as reasons for individuals to accept the belief or theory in question. Examples of these factors include experimental reports, successful predictions, background theories, generalizations drawn from experience, and other such things that function to epistemi-cally support the belief or theory in question. In the words of Ernan

McMullin, one of the active participants in this debate, epistemic factors are 'those sorts of considerations that would weigh with a contemporary scientist who might be repeating the earlier work or discussing it in a science course'.[62] Non-epistemic factors include, on the other hand, such things as social, political or psychological considerations.

Since the present work is concerned with the relationship between Hobbes's political ideas, which include non-epistemic factors, and his natural philosophy, which is supposed to be grounded on epistemic considerations, the sociology of knowledge debate hovers in the background. In recent research on the sociology of knowledge, one finds three types of answers to the question why scientists accept the beliefs and theories that they do. First, there is the view that non-epistemic factors are mostly, if not entirely, responsible for explaining the acceptance of scientific beliefs. According to advocates of what is called the 'strong programme in the sociology of knowledge', social causes are granted priority in the explanation of scientific belief. David Bloor, one of the leading advocates of the strong programme, claims the 'sociologist seeks theories which explain the beliefs which are in fact found, regardless of how the investigator evaluates them'.[63] For Bloor, the evaluation of a belief does not really play a role in the explanation of its adoption, except insofar as evaluative standards are themselves revelatory of social and other non-epistemic factors.

Second, there is the view, which I call the 'rationality program', that epistemic factors should be given priority in the explanation of scientific rationality. When understanding why a scientist holds a particular belief, one should simply consider the reasons supporting the belief in question. If epistemic factors alone provide an adequate explanation, that is, if the rationality of the belief is revealed, then the scientific belief has been explained and there is no need to delve further into other, non-epistemic factors. According to what has been called the 'arationality assumption', one should appeal to non-epistemic factors only in those cases where epistemic factors fail to provide a good explanation for the belief. Larry Lauden, who is responsible for coining the term, describes the arationality assumption in the following way:

Essentially, the arationality assumption establishes a division of labor between the historian of ideas and the sociologist of knowledge; saying, in effect, that the historian of ideas, using the machinery available to him, can explain the history of thought insofar as it is rationally well-founded and that the sociologist of knowledge steps in at precisely those points where a rational analysis of the acceptance (or rejection) of an idea fails to square with the actual situation.[64]

The priority of the rationality position, then, employs non-epistemic factors in special circumstances.

Third, one may take a middle path and deny the priority of either epistemic or non-epistemic factors in explaining scientific belief. According to what I call the 'neutral programme', a complete explanation involves an appeal to both epistemic and non-epistemic factors, neither of which is given priority. Thus, even in cases where a scientific belief can be explained by either epistemic or non-epistemic factors alone, the advocate of the neutral programme claims that a complete account requires a revelation of all the factors at work. Ernan McMullin, for example, advocates the neutral programme when he claims that 'what is needed is a detailed and historically sensitive analysis of reasons and motives, in which the status of neither the rational nor the social is ever taken for granted'.[65] Non-epistemic factors are not called in simply when the rationality of a belief is difficult or impossible to discern.

One should note that the contrast between the philosophical and the political interpretive approaches (discussed in Section 1.1.a) finds an interesting parallel in the sociology of knowledge debate. For the most part, Hobbes scholars have traditionally adopted an approach that falls within the confines of the rationality programme.

As we have seen, advocates of the philosophical approach disregard sociological and other non-epistemic factors in their attempt at a rational reconstruction of Hobbes's philosophical arguments. For these scholars, non-epistemic factors, if appealed to at all, are used primarily to provide a context for Hobbes's thought, not as a mode for *explaining* his beliefs. On the other hand, advocates of the political approach, as do advocates of the strong programme, operate under the assumption that non-epistemic factors play a primary role in the explanation of Hobbes's beliefs. The fundamental aim of the present work is to show that Hobbes's political ideas play an influential role in his natural philosophy, to the point where non-epistemic factors must be used to better understand Hobbes's natural philosophy.

Since I plan to reveal the influence of Hobbes's political ideas on his natural philosophy, and since Hobbes's political ideas include his political agenda, I need to employ non-epistemic factors in interpreting his philosophy. As shall be shown, my primary method for revealing this influence is to show that Hobbes has strong *political* reasons to *accept* certain 'strictly philosophical' views, even though he has strong *philosophical* reasons to *reject* these views. This unveils a tension between Hobbes's political and scientific goal that, as I will argue, results in obvious inconsistencies in his natural philosophy. By showing a pattern of such tensions and inconsistencies, then, I will attempt to support the thesis of a political influence. If it is true that Hobbes's political aims play an influential role in his natural philosophy, then a proper understanding of his natural philosophy requires us to appeal to more than just the scientific reasons that led Hobbes to adopt certain beliefs or theories in natural philosophy. I accept such an approach because of my conviction that one must use all the resources at one's disposal to arrive at a better understanding of Hobbes's natural philosophy. One might object that such an approach is not philosophical and is best left to historians or sociologists; however, not only do non-epistemic factors play a role by enhancing our understanding of Hobbes's *philosophy*, I shall argue, but such factors often contribute to a resolution of philosophical inconsistencies in his philosophy. Employing the arationality assumption, then, it is possible to explain certain problematic features in Hobbes's philosophy by appealing to non-epistemic factors. Since this is the case, an interpretive approach that includes non-epistemic considerations does have a philosophical role to play.

1.2 Outline of the Chapters

This work consists of seven chapters, including this one. In the second chapter, I provide an account of what I call the 'traditional interpretation of influence'. According to this interpretation, Hobbes's discovery of geometry and his interest in natural philosophy play an important role in shaping his political philosophy. I present this account not only to offer an informational backdrop for the following investigation, but also to provide a point of contrast between my interpretation and the traditional one. The chapter begins with an overview of the main elements of Hobbes's philosophy, which is followed by an account of the influence of natural philosophy on political philosophy.

The third chapter, introducing Hobbes's political agenda, includes a discussion of the political and historical context within which he was writing. In this chapter, I argue that Hobbes's political agenda formed early in his philosophical career and remained fairly consistent throughout his life. An investigation into his works shows that Hobbes's political philosophy from start to finish was aimed at specific opponents, among whom I number religious leaders, Aristotelians and common law lawyers.

In the remaining chapters, I support the thesis of a political influence in Hobbes's natural philosophy. In Chapter 4, I discuss the ways in which Hobbes's political philosophy enables his philosophy of mind and his mechanistic materialism. I will show that Hobbes's mechanistic and materialist description of mental phenomena has important political implications, implications suggesting that he may have been politically motivated to accept specific psychological notions. In Chapter 5, I present Hobbes's view of truth and reveal some of the inconsistencies within it. More specifically, I show that although Hobbes explicitly adheres to the conventional view of truth, he frequently makes claims that are inconsistent with this view. I also argue that attempts at resolving these inconsistencies do not succeed. A political influence, I further suggest, provides us with a good explanation for the inconsistencies in Hobbes's view of truth. According to this suggestion, there is a pattern of political influence showing that Hobbes *accepts* specific positions in natural philosophy that he has good scientific or logical reasons to *reject*. In Chapters 6 and 7, I further defend my thesis by revealing a political influence at work in Hobbes's views of nominalism and reason, respectively. In these cases, again, one sees that Hobbes has strong political reasons to accept 'strictly' philosophical views, although he has good philosophical reasons to reject these views. Inconsistencies arise in Hobbes's natural philosophy, in others words, because political concerns influence him to accept views that he has logical reasons to deny. At the end of Chapter 7, I conclude the work by defending my interpretation as the best among competing alternatives.

Notes

1. Aubrey, J. (1972), *Aubrey's Brief Lives*. O. L. Dick (ed.) Harmondsworth: Penguin, p. 230.
2. The debate about the authorship and dating of the 'Short Tract on First Principles' will be discussed in Chapter 2.
3. Steinberg, J. (1988), *The Obsession of Thomas Hobbes: The English Civil War in Hobbes's Political Philosophy*. New York: Peter Lang.
4. Warrender, H. (1957), *The Political Philosophy of Hobbes: His Theory of Obligation*. Oxford: Clarendon Press, p. 3.
5. Ibid., p. 240.
6. Ibid., pp. 240–1.

7. Plamenatz, J. P. (1963), *Man and Society: Political and Social Theory: Machiavelli through Rousseau.* Vol. 1. New York: McGraw-Hill Book Company, p. ix. Quoted in Steinberg, *The Obsession of Thomas Hobbes*, p. 6.
8. Ibid.
9. de Crespigny, A. and Minogue, K. (1975), 'Introduction', in A. de Crespigny and K. Minogue (eds), *Contemporary Political Philosophy.* New York: Mead and Company, p. xii. Quoted in Steinberg, *The Obsession of Thomas Hobbes*, p. 2.
10. Kavka, G. (1986), *Hobbesian Moral and Political Theory.* Princeton, NJ: Princeton University Press, p. 4.
11. Ibid.
12. See also Gauthier, D. (1969), *The Logic of Leviathan: The Moral and Political Theory of Thomas Hobbes.* Oxford: Clarendon Press.
13. Steinberg, *The Obsession of Thomas Hobbes*, pp. 2–3.
14. Ibid., p. 3.
15. Ibid.
16. Ibid., pp. 15–16.
17. Ibid., p. 14.
18. Ibid., p. 17.
19. Ibid., p. ix.
20. Ibid., p. 15.
21. Skinner, Q. (1996), *Reason and Rhetoric in the Philosophy of Hobbes.* Cambridge: Cambridge University Press, p. 10.
22. Watkins, J. (1965), *Hobbes's System of Ideas.* London: Hutchinson & Co., p. 10.
23. Ibid., p.1. My emphasis.
24. Skinner, *Reason and Rhetoric*, p. 10.
25. Martinich, A. P. (1992), *The Two Gods of Leviathan.* Cambridge: Cambridge University Press, p. 11.
26. Ibid., p. 12.
27. Ibid.
28. For good works on Hobbes from a strictly historical perspective see Sommerville, J. P. (1992), *Thomas Hobbes: Political Ideas in Historical Context.* London: MacMillan; Rogow, A. A. (1986), *Thomas Hobbes: Radical in the Service of Reaction.* New York: W. W. Norton & Company.
29. Martinich, *The Two Gods of Leviathan*, p. 11.
30. See, for example, Herbert, G. (1989), *Thomas Hobbes: The Unity of Scientific and Moral Wisdom.* Vancouver: University of British Columbia Press; Goldsmith, M. M. (1966), *Hobbes's Science of Politics.* New York:

Columbia University Press; Watkins, *Hobbes's System*.
31. See, for example, Sorell, T. (1986), *Hobbes*. London: Routledge and Kegan Paul; Shelton, G. (1992), *Morality and Sovereignty in the Philosophy of Hobbes*. New York: St Martin's Press.
32. Gauthier, *The Logic of Leviathan*, p. 3.
33. Macpherson, C. B. (1968), 'Introduction to *Leviathan*', in Hobbes, T., *Leviathan*. C. B. Macpherson (ed.) Harmondsworth: Penguin, p. 27.
34. Berns, L. (1987), 'Thomas Hobbes', in L. Strauss and J. Cropsey (eds), *History of Political Philosophy*. Chicago, IL: University of Chicago Press, p. 397.
35. Herbert, *The Unity of Scientific and Moral Wisdom*, p. x.
36. Robert Russell, for example: 'Thus, with the supposition that only bodies exist, together with the mechanical interpretation of their activity according to the theories of Galileo, Hobbes sets about to deduce in Euclidean fashion a system of philosophy from these first principles. This philosophy of "body" and "motion" is all comprehensive; beginning with the investigation of what effects are caused by a body in simple motion and extending to an inquiry of the motions of man which are the cause of political society.' See Russell, R. (1939), *Natural Law in the Philosophy of Thomas Hobbes*. Dissertation for the Doctorate in the Faculty of Philosophy of the Pontifical Gregorian University. See also Goldsmith, *Hobbes's Science of Politics*: 'From the definitions and explications of the fundamental principles of science (place, motion, cause, etc.), the effects of the various motions are deduced (mechanics). This is followed by an investigation of sense and its causes. Next come the science of human passion and action – psychology in the widest sense – and finally civil philosophy, the science of natural justice' (pp. 10–11). Similar views are also found in Curley, E. (1994), 'Introduction to Hobbes's *Leviathan*', in E. Curley (ed.), *Leviathan*. Indianapolis, IN: Hackett Publishing, pp. viii–ix; David Gauthier, *The Logic of Leviathan*, pp. 1–26.
37. Watkins, *Hobbes's System*, p. 5.
38. Ibid., p. 1.
39. Michael Oakeshott apparently offers another version of the systematic interpretation when he claims that one must search for the 'unity' of Hobbes's thinking. Instead of finding this unity in a scientific deduction, Oakeshott discovers it in a single 'passionate thought' that ties all the elements together: 'The coherence of his philosophy, the system of it, lies not in its architectonic structure, but in a single 'passionate thought' that

pervades its parts.' According to Oakeshott, 'the system of Hobbes's philosophy lies in his conception of the nature of philosophical knowledge' and the 'inspiration of philosophy is the intention to be guided by reason and to reject all other guides'. This intention does not seem to me to be enough to call Hobbes's philosophy a 'system', except in a loose sense. A 'system' implies a collection of parts that function together and, in some sense, rely upon each other to function. See Oakeshott, M. (1962), *Hobbes on Civil Association*. New York: Cromwell-Collier, p. 16.

40. Strauss, L. (1952), *The Political Philosophy of Hobbes: Its Basis and Its Genesis*. Chicago, IL: University of Chicago Press, p. 7.
41. Sorell, *Hobbes*, p. 4.
42. Gert, B. (1965b), 'Hobbes, Mechanism, and Egoism', *Philosophy Quarterly*, 15, 341.
43. Ibid.
44. McNeilly, F. S. (1968), *The Anatomy of Leviathan*. London: St Martin's Press, p. 95.
45. Watkins, *Hobbes's System of Ideas*, p. 43. My emphasis.
46. Ibid., p. 1.
47. Strauss, *The Political Philosophy of Hobbes*, p. 2.
48. Quoted in ibid., p. xiii.
49. Lynch, W. T. (1991), 'Politics in Hobbes's Mechanics: The Social as Enabling', *Studies in the History of the Philosophy of Science*, 22, (2), 296.
50. Ibid., pp. 297–8.
51. Shapin, S. and Shapiro, S. (1985), *Leviathan and the Air-Pump: Hobbes, Boyle, and the Experimental Life*. Princeton, NJ: Princeton University Press.
52. Lynch, 'Politics in Hobbes's Mechanics', p. 297.
53. Ibid., p. 296.
54. Shapin and Shapiro, *Leviathan and the Air-Pump*, p. 13. Quoted in Lynch, 'Politics in Hobbes's Mechanics', p. 296.
55. Lynch, 'Politics in Hobbes's Mechanics', p. 296.
56. Ibid.
57. Ibid., p. 297.
58. Ibid.
59. Ibid., p. 319.
60. Ibid.
61. Ibid., pp. 298–9.
62. McMullin, E. (1984), 'The Rational and the Social in the History of Science', in J. R. Brown (ed.), *Scientific Rationality: The Sociological Turn*.

Dordrecht: D. Reidel Publishing Company, p. 130.

63. Bloor, D. (1976), *Knowledge and Social Imagery*. London: Routledge and Kegan Paul, p. 3.

64. Laudan, L. (1977), *Progress and Its Problems*. Berkeley, CA: University of California Press, p. 202.

65. McMullin, 'The Rational and the Social', p. 159.

2

The Traditional Interpretation of Influence

2.0 Introduction

Scholars commonly recognize that the development of Hobbes's moral and political philosophy was dramatically influenced by the emergence of a new scientific worldview. Hobbes was a witness to numerous developments in all areas of scientific research in the seventeenth century. In the early 1600s, for example, the Scotsman John Napier invented the mathematical technique of logarithms, which reduced the operations of multiplication and division to addition and subtraction. This technique allowed for the easy calculations of large numbers, such as those employed in astronomy. Descartes' advances in analytical geometry were applied to nature in the new mechanical physical sciences. Theoretical achievements were accompanied by the introduction of scientific instruments that were themselves either newly created or put to novel uses; telescopes, microscopes, thermometers, barometers and the air pump were all used to investigate natural phenomena. Galileo, for example, supported the Copernican theory of celestial motions with empirical data provided by the telescope. Francis Bacon, who was Hobbes's employer for a short time, stressed the importance of experiment and the systematic use of empirical information in establishing scientific theories. The creation of scientific societies, such as the Royal Society of London and the Academie Royale des Sciences of Paris, further encouraged the growth of scientific knowledge.

Given the scientific spirit of the age and his interest in both political and natural philosophy, it is not surprising that Hobbes sought to establish a science of politics. A desire to create a science of politics along the lines of geometry permeates all three of Hobbes's major political works. *The Elements of Law*, circulating in manuscript form in 1640, is Hobbes's first attempt at writing a scientific political treatise. In the Epistle Dedicatory of this work, Hobbes claims there are two types of learning: 'mathematical' and 'dogmatical'. Mathematical learning is 'free from controversies and dispute because it consisteth in comparing figures and motion only; in which things truth and the interest of men oppose not each other' (*El* Epistle. xv). In dogmatical learning, by contrast, 'there is nothing not disputable, because it compareth men, and meddleth with their right and profit' (*El* Epistle. xv). Previous political writers, Hobbes claims, are not only dogmatic, but they 'invade each other, and themselves, with contradiction' (*El* Epistle. xv). Hobbes's own political philosophy is supposed to be modelled on geometry, a science responsible for numerous benefits. 'Whatsoever things they are in which this present age doth differ from the rude simpleness of antiquity,' Hobbes says, is a 'debt which we owe merely to geometry' (*Ci* Dedication. 91). A civil philosophy modelled on geometry, like geometry itself, would also produce beneficial consequences, the most important of which is a state of 'immortal peace' (*Ci* Dedication. 91). Previous philosophers have been unable to establish a science of politics because they have not started with an 'idoneous principle of tractation' (*Ci* Dedication. 92). The success of geometry, in part, comes from the fact that anyone can know its foundational principles. In *De Cive*, Hobbes offers a primary principle for his civil philosophy that is 'by experience known to all men and denied by none' (*Ci* Preface. 99). With such a principle in place, Hobbes believes he can 'demonstrate by a most evident connexion' the conclusions of science of politics (*Ci* Preface. 93).

Hobbes's desire to create a science of politics reveals one of the fundamental tenets of what I call the 'traditional interpretation of influence', namely, that the discovery of geometry influenced his approach to political philosophy.[1] This is just one example of how Hobbes's natural philosophy plays an influential role in his political philosophy. As mentioned in Chapter 1, the overwhelming majority of Hobbes scholars choose one of two options when relating his natural philosophy to his political philosophy. The systematic interpreters, on the one hand, believe the premises of political philosophy are taken from the conclusions of natural philosophy. The non-systematic interpreters, on the other hand, often claim Hobbes's political argument is grounded on empirical principles concerning human nature. Despite their differences, adherents on both sides have correctly recognized the important influence of natural philosophy on Hobbes's political philosophy, but have overlooked the manner in which his political ideas have, in turn, influenced his natural philosophy. In this chapter, I will summarize the traditional interpretation of influence by revealing how Hobbes's natural philosophy influences his political philosophy, regardless of whether the two are independent. In the process, I will also lay the groundwork for the defence of my thesis by providing an overview of the main elements of Hobbes's philosophy.[2]

This chapter contains five sections. Section 2.1 provides a brief summary of Hobbes's early thoughts on natural philosophy. In Section 2.2, I outline Hobbes's mature natural philosophy as found in *De Corpore*. The traditional interpretation of influence is then described in Section 2.3. The following section uses *Leviathan* as an example to further elaborate upon, and provide evidence for, the traditional interpretation of influence. Concluding remarks will then be made in Section 2.5.

2.1 The 'Short Tract': Hobbes's Early Thoughts on Natural Philosophy

According to his autobiography, Hobbes discovered the importance of Euclid's geometry while in Geneva on his first tour of the continent in 1630 (*OL* xxxviii). Certainly, Hobbes had been exposed to scientific issues earlier in his life. In the 1620s, for example, he served as secretary to Francis Bacon, one of the most important scientific figures of the time. Nevertheless, Hobbes's fascination with natural philosophy probably did not extend beyond geometry into other issues until 1634. In the autumn of that year, Hobbes began his third tour of the continent, during which tour he would meet and converse with leading intellectuals, including Galileo, Marin Mersenne, Rene Descartes and Pierre Gassendi. It was probably during this time that Hobbes became seriously interested in scientific questions about the physical world and, more specifically, about the mechanical causes of sensation.[3]

Some scholars believe Hobbes's first work on natural philosophy is 'A Short Tract on First Principles', probably written sometime between 1630 and 1636. Ferdinand Tonnies, for example, suggests that Hobbes composed this work as early as 1630.[4] The primary form of evidence for this dating is Hobbes's own claim of having offered in 1630 a mechanical description of sensation. William Lynch, however, disputes Tonnies' suggestion partly because the descriptive comments made by Hobbes do not match the specific position advanced in the 'Short Tract'.[5] On the basis of a series of Hobbes's letters, Lynch argues that it is 'implausible that Hobbes had any kind of worked out view in natural philosophy until 1636 at the earliest, unless the "Little Treatise" [i.e., "Short Tract"] was in fact written by Hobbes'.[6] Lynch admits that 'Hobbes might have mentioned the concept of motion explaining light and heat as early as 1630 as he claimed', but this does not mean Hobbes authored the 'Short Tract'.[7] Richard Tuck also believes Hobbes is not the author since the handwriting of the tract resembles Payne's handwriting rather than Hobbes's. Tuck further claims the 'Short Tract' contains too much Aristotelianism to be the work of Hobbes.[8] A. P. Martinich, taking a more cautious approach to the matter, believes the 'Short Tract' provides insight into the early thought of Hobbes, even if it is not the actual product of the philosopher, since the work provides a glimpse into the type of thinking characteristic of Hobbes's philosophical associates.[9] In my remarks on the 'Short Tract', I will assume the soundness of Martinich's view since most interpreters attribute the ideas of the 'Short Tract', if not the authorship of it, to Hobbes.

A brief investigation of the 'Short Tract' reveals both similarities and differences with Hobbes's mature thoughts. In the following remarks, I focus on three similarities: (1) the influence of geometry on philosophical methodology, (2) a mechanistic account of nature and of human nature, and (3) an account of the good in terms of appetite. In each of these cases, as we shall see, the author of the 'Short Tract' provides rudimentary versions of Hobbes's later views. In the first case, the 'Short Tract' reveals an influence of geometry on philosophical method. The 'Short Tract' is divided into three sections, each of which contains a list of principles followed by a list of conclusions supposedly drawn from the principles. The tract therefore reveals a commitment to a methodology that deduces conclusions from foundational principles. In the second case, the 'Short Tract' provides a mechanistic account of motion that accepts the primacy of efficient causality and denies the concept of self-motion. The author claims in the conclusions of the first section that 'nothing can move it self' (*ST* 1.196). 'That which now resteth', the author concludes, 'cannot be moved, unless it be touched by some Agent' (*ST* 1.195). Unfortunately, the mechanistic account of motion is clouded by the mention of an Aristotelian 'active power' within the agent itself. For example, one of the principles in this work asserts that 'whatsoever move another, moveth either by active power inherent in itself, or by motion received from another' (*ST* 1.193).[10] The 'Short Tract', in the third case, provides a subjective view of the good. In this work, the good is 'to every thing, that which hath active power to attract it locally' (*ST* 3.208). The author also defines the good by relating it to desire: 'Whatsoever is Good is desirable; and whatsoever is desirable is Good' (*ST* 3.208). Since the good is defined in terms of desires, the subjectivity of the good seems to follow naturally. 'Because that which is desirable or good to one', the author says, 'may not be so to another, and so what attracts one, may not attract another' (*ST* 3.209). These three views, as we shall see, are all rudimentary versions of positions in Hobbes's mature natural philosophy.

2.2 *De Corpore*: Hobbes's Mature Thoughts on Natural Philosophy

Hobbes's most extensive text on natural philosophy, *De Corpore*, was published in 1655. The treatise is divided into four parts: (I) Logic or Computation, (II) The First Grounds of Philosophy, (III) Proportions of Magnitudes and Motions, (IV) Physics, or the Phenomena of Nature. In Part I, Hobbes specifies the various aspects of his philosophical methodology. Part II addresses the most general conceptions that accompany our ideas of bodies: space, time, quantity, proportion, angle and figure. Part III is concerned with abstract magnitude and motion, which 'are the most common accidents of all bodies' and 'therefore most properly belong to the elements of geometry' (*Co* 15.203). In Part IV, Hobbes offers his physical investigations of the natural world. In the following sections, I discuss some of the main components of Hobbes's natural philosophy, in order of their appearance in *De Corpore*.

2.2.a Philosophical Method

At the start of Chapter 1 of *De Corpore*, which is entitled 'Of Philosophy', Hobbes uses an analogy to emphasize the importance of philosophical method for acquiring scientific knowledge.[11] Philosophy, he says, seems 'to be amongst men now, in the same manner as corn and wine are said to have been in ancient times' (*Co* 1.1). In earlier days, vines and ears of corn were naturally scattered about in the fields, yet no one had taken pains to plant and sow them. Until such pains were taken, humans sustained themselves by eating acorns, unaware of the benefits of the planting and sowing of corn. Similarly, humans were endowed with the natural faculty of reasoning which, had it been improved, would have allowed them to avoid errors and mistakes. 'Most men wander out of the way,' Hobbes remarks, 'and fall into error for want of method, as it were for want of sowing and planting' (*Co* 1.1–2). Those who are content with exercising their natural reason, without improving it in any way, 'do nothing but dispute and wrangle, like men that are not in their wits' (*Co* 1.2). The lesson to be learned here is that a proper philosophical method allows individuals not only to dodge error, but also disputes.

Philosophical knowledge, according to Hobbes, is an acquired form of knowledge that begins with raw material provided by the senses. Hobbes states the 'first beginnings of knowledge' are the 'phantasms of sense and imagination' (*Co* 6.66). Sensation is itself a kind of knowledge: 'Sense and Memory of things, which are common to man and all living creatures, be knowledge' (*Co* 1.3). Sense knowledge, however, is not philosophical because it is 'given immediately by nature, and not gotten by ratiocination' (*Co* 1.3). Philosophical knowledge, unlike that of brute sensations, is acquired by an act of reason, a faculty that 'computes' ideas by the operations of addition or subtraction (*Co* 1.3). To explain how reason adds and subtracts ideas, Hobbes employs the example of the perception of a man far off in the distance. According to this example, upon perceiving a man far away, you first perceive him as a 'body.' When the man comes closer, you see the body is animated, so reason 'adds' the notion of 'animation' to the notion of 'body'. Finally, when you see the animated body speaking and acting like a rational creature, reason adds the notion of 'rational' to the conceptions of 'animated' and 'body'.

Lastly, when by looking fully and distinctly upon it, he conceives all that he has seen as one thing, the idea he has now is

compounded of his former ideas which are put together in the
mind in the same order in which these three single names, *body*,
animated, *rational*, are in speech compounded into this one name,
body-animated-rational, or *man*. (*Co* 1.4)

The operation of subtraction functions in a similar manner since if
the man walks away you would first 'lose the idea of those things
which were signs of his being rational' and then you would
'subtract' the idea of animation as well (*Co* 1.5). The operations of
addition and subtraction, when employed in philosophical investigation, are called 'composition' and 'resolution'.

The subject matter of philosophy, according to Hobbes, is 'every
body of which we can conceive any generation' and 'which is
capable of composition and resolution' (*Co* 1.10). In relation to the
resolution and composition of bodies, for example, resolution is the
intellectual process of dismantling a whole into its parts. Composition refers to the contrary movement of constructing a whole from
its parts. As in the example above, the idea of the whole man is
resolved into its parts, and the parts are composed to produce the
idea of the man. Hobbes believes that knowledge of the
composition and resolution is philosophical because it captures
the fundamental properties of bodies. If a circle is placed before us,
Hobbes illustrates, 'we cannot possibly perceive by sense whether it
be a circle or no' (*Co* 1.6). Yet, if it is 'known that the figure was
made by the circumduction of a body whereof one end remained
unmoved', we will know that all the radii are equal (*Co* 1.6).
Similarly, if we know the figure is a circle, 'we may come by
ratiocination to some generation of the same' (*Co* 1.6).

We should note that Hobbes refers to the movements of
philosophical method not only with the paired terms of parts and
wholes, but also with the paired terms of cause/effect and
generation/appearance. Hobbes defines philosophy, for example,
as 'such knowledge of effects or appearances, as we acquire by true
ratiocination from the knowledge we have first of their causes or

generation: And again, of such causes or generations as may be from knowing their effects' (*Co* 1.3). To resolve a body into its constituent parts is to reveal its causes, which are responsible for its generation. One discovers, in other words, those things that, when compounded together, cause the effect or the appearance of the body in question.

While Chapter 1 of *De Corpore* primarily concerns the nature of philosophical method, the chapter also includes observations on the end, the scope, the utility and the branches of philosophy. The end of philosophical knowledge, Hobbes claims, is power (*Co* 1.7). Although Hobbes does not expand upon the notion of power here, he does say that philosophical knowledge for its own sake 'is not worth so much pains as the study of Philosophy requires' (*Co* 1.7).[12] The pragmatic nature of philosophical investigation is an important aspect of philosophy for Hobbes. He confirms this when he defines the 'scope of all speculation' as the 'performance of some action, or thing to be done' (*Co* 1.7). The utility of philosophy is 'best understood by reckoning up the chief commodities of which mankind is capable, and by comparing the manner of life of such as enjoy them, with the others which want the same' (*Co* 1.7). Such a comparison shows that philosophical knowledge has significant practical benefits (*Co* 1.7).

2.2.b Philosophy of Language and Scientific Demonstration

The introductory comments on the nature of philosophical method provided in Chapter 1 of *De Corpore* are followed, in Chapters 2 through 4, by an in-depth discussion of language and its role in philosophical methodology.[13] In these chapters, Hobbes slowly composes his definition of scientific demonstration, which is a *'syllogism or a series of syllogisms, derived and continued, from the definitions of names, to the last conclusion'* (*Co* 6.86). The definition is progressively constructed in Chapters 2, 3 and 4, which are respectively entitled 'Of Names', 'Of Propositions' and 'Of

Syllogism'. Names, Hobbes says, are 'marks' used to recall certain thoughts to our minds (*Co* 2.17). When names are employed to communicate our thoughts to others, they function as 'signs of our conceptions' (*Co* 2.17). A name, in other words, is used either as a mnemonic device for oneself or as a means to signify to others the conceptions that exist in one's own mind. When two names are joined by a copula a proposition is created. According to Hobbes, a 'proposition is a speech consisting of two names copulated, by which he that speaketh signifies he conceives the latter name to be the name of the thing whereof the former is the name' (*Co* 3.30). In the proposition 'man is a living creature', for example, 'he that speaks it conceives both *living creature* and *man* to be names of the same thing' (*Co* 3.30). In *Leviathan*, Hobbes defines power as the 'present means to obtain some future apparent good' (*L* 10.150). Propositions are the fundamental elements of syllogisms. A syllogism, Hobbes says, is a 'speech consisting of three propositions, from two of which the third follows' (*Co* 4.44).

With the definition of syllogism in place, Hobbes defines scientific demonstration as an activity of constructing syllogisms or a series of syllogisms. For Hobbes, a scientific demonstration is a syllogism that produces true and universal conclusions. In Chapter 6 of *De Corpore*, for example, Hobbes claims that 'all true ratiocination which taketh its beginnings from true principles, produceth science, and is true demonstration' (*Co* 6.86). It is important that the premises of a scientific demonstration are certainly known, since its conclusion can only be as certain as the premises from which it is derived: 'For there can be no certainty of the last conclusion, without a certainty of all those Affirmations and Negations, on which it was grounded, and inferred' (*L* 5.112). In geometry, which is Hobbes's paradigm of scientific demonstration, the 'truth of the first principles of our ratiocination, namely definitions, is made and constituted by ourselves, whilst we consent and agree about the appellations of things' (*Co* 25.388). Hobbes suggests a conventional view of truth, according to which the truth of propositions is established by human agreement.[14] In addition to truth, another required characteristic of scientific demonstration is 'universality'. In the process of differentiating between positive and negative affirmations, Hobbes declares it is the 'profession' of philosophy (or science, since the two are interchangeable) to 'establish *universal* rules concerning the properties of things' (*Co* 4.49). A demonstration involving singular names, therefore, is 'useless in philosophy' even if it is a valid demonstration (*Co* 4.46). According to Hobbes, universal names are necessary for science since they allow of no exceptions. If 'man is a rational, animated body' is true, then the terms 'rational', 'animated' and 'body' are predicated of *all* men. A scientific demonstration, then, is a syllogism that begins with true and universal principles and, on the basis of these, validly deduces conclusions with the same characteristics.[15]

2.2.c The Science of Motion

The study of philosophy, Hobbes says, proceeds in a 'simple' or 'indefinite' manner (*Co* 6.68). To inquire into the causes of a specific phenomenon or to answer a determinate question is to pursue science simply. In this endeavour one may employ either a synthetic or a resolutive method. To 'search after science indefinitely', on the other hand, is to seek 'knowledge of the causes of all things' and of the 'accidents that are common to all things' (*Co* 6.68). Such investigation utilizes the resolutive method because it resolves bodies into their ultimate parts, i.e., those parts that are common to all bodies.

> Moreover, seeing universal things are contained in the nature of singular things, the knowledge of them is to be acquired by reason, that is, by resolution. For example, if there be propounded a conception or *idea* of some singular thing, as of a *square*, this square is to be resolved into *plain, terminated with a*

certain number of equal and straight lines and right angles. For by this
resolution we have these things universal or agreeable to all
matter, namely, *line, plain, (which contains superficies) terminated,
angle, straightness, rectitude and equality*; and if we can find the causes
of these, we may compound them altogether into the cause of a
square. (*Co* 6.69–70)

A continual resolution reveals that these universal things 'have but
one universal cause, which is motion' (*Co* 6.69). This is due to the
fact that the 'variety of all figures arises out of the variety of those
motions by which they are made; and motion cannot be understood
to have any other cause besides motion' (*Co* 6.69–70).

The various branches of Hobbes's philosophy, then, are all
sciences of motion.[16] Hobbes believes, for example, that geometry
is a science of motion because it is concerned with the construction
of figures through the motion of points: 'a line is made by the
motion of a point, superficies by the motion of a line, and one
motion by another motion, &c' (*Co* 6.70–1). The science of physics
is an 'enquiry of such effects as are made by the motion of the parts
of any body' (*Co* 6.72). Moral philosophy is concerned with the
'motions of the mind, namely, appetite, aversion, love, benevolence, hope, fear, anger, emulation, envy, &c.; what causes they
have and of what they be causes' (*Co* 6.72). By understanding the
motions of the mind, Hobbes claims, one can discover the motions,
or changes, by which a commonwealth is created. The 'principles of
politics', according to Hobbes, 'consist in the knowledge of the
motions of the mind' (*Co* 6.74). In all of these cases, the subject
matter of investigation is a certain form of motion.

2.2.d Geometry and Physics

After describing the main elements of his philosophical methodology in Part I of *De Corpore*, the synthetic side of this method is
applied in Parts II and III. In Part II, Hobbes presents a number of

foundational definitions, including those of space, time and bodies, which he uses to construct an abstract world of geometric figures. Parts II and III of *De Corpore* discuss abstract bodies, defined as having an independent existence from us, but which are ultimately part of a constructed world. At the end of Part III, where Hobbes finishes his geometry and begins his physics, the investigation shifts away from the abstract world to the 'real and existent' one:

> And here I put an end to the third part of this discourse; in which I have considered motion and magnitude by themselves in the abstract. The fourth and last part, concerning the *phenomena of nature*, that is to say, concerning the motions and magnitudes of the bodies which are parts of the world, real and existent, is that which follows. (*Co* 24.386)

Since Part IV investigates bodies existing in the real world, the movement from Parts III to IV marks a transition from geometry to physics.

At the start of Part IV, Hobbes reiterates the point that philosophical knowledge is acquired via a compositive or a resolutive method. In the present context, however, Hobbes claims the resolutive method, which is the method used in physics, proceeds from 'effects or appearances [of things] to some possible generation of the same' (*Co* 25.388).[17] The goal of physics, accordingly, is to discover the causes responsible for the 'appearances' or phantasms of natural bodies. Since this search must begin with the phantasms themselves, Hobbes believes the first job of physics is to analyse the faculty of sense wherein they reside: 'And as for the causes of sense, we cannot begin our search of them from any other phenomenon than that of sense itself' (*Co* 25.389). In one way, sense is the most fundamental physical principle, for without it, there could be no phantasms whatsoever: 'So that if appearances be the principles by which we know all other things, we must needs acknowledge sense to be the principle by which we know those

principles, and that all the knowledge we have is derived from it'
(*Co* 25.389).

Hobbes's physics incorporates a resolution of both human
sensation and natural bodies. Human sensation is first resolved into
its various 'parts': the sense organs, the faculties of imagination and
fancy, and the sensations of pleasure and pain.[18] After sense, natural
bodies are resolved: 'Consequent to the contemplation of sense is
the contemplation of bodies, which are the efficient causes or
objects of sense' (*Co* 26.410). In keeping with the resolutive
method, the investigation of natural bodies starts by a resolution of
the 'whole' world: 'Now every object is either a part of the whole
world, or an aggregate of parts. The greatest of all bodies, or sensible
objects, is the world itself' (*Co* 26.410). Beginning with the whole
world, Hobbes attempts to uncover the variety of motions that are
responsible for physical phenomena. In relation to motions in the
natural world, Hobbes searches for the causes of a variety of physical
phenomena, such as the motion of the stars, the change of seasons,
the presence of heat and colour, and the power of gravity. All
natural phenomena are ultimately explained, just as geometric
figures are, in terms of bodies in motion.

An important difference between the compositive and the
resolutive method used in geometry and physics, respectively,
concerns the epistemological status of their results. Geometry, as we
have seen, operates within the realm of truth because it is grounded
on primary principles, or definitions, that are known as true because
we construct them. The principles of physics, on the other hand,
'are not such as we make and pronounce in general terms, as
definitions; but such as being placed in things themselves by the
Author of Nature, are by us observed in them' (*Co* 25.388). Since
physical objects are not 'constituted' by humans, but are known
through observation, physics relies on hypothetical reasoning.
Physics, Hobbes says, 'depends upon hypotheses; which unless
we know them to be true, it is impossible for us to demonstrate that
those causes, which I have there explicated, are the true causes' (*Co*

30.531). Thus, the conclusions of physics cannot be demonstrated as true since we cannot know that the primary principles are true. This is due to the fact that we do not create the primary principles, but seek them through resolution, that is, we discover causes through effects: 'But because of natural bodies we know not the construction, but seek it from the effects, there lies no demonstration of what the causes be we seek for, but only of what they *may* be' (*EW* 7.184). The difference in the demonstrable nature of physics and geometry is ultimately based upon their contrasting methodologies.

2.3 The Traditional Interpretation of Influence

In *De Cive*, Hobbes tell us that the turmoil of the times forced him to publish his political philosophy before his natural philosophy, even though the latter is supposed to be logically and systematically prior to the former. Although *De Corpore* was published after the writing of his three main political treatises, there are still obvious ways in which his political philosophy is infiltrated by his scientific views on natural philosophy. Adherents of the traditional interpretation find two important strands of influence of Hobbes's natural philosophy on his political philosophy.[19] In the first case, Hobbes's 'science of motion' guides his view of human nature and subsequently his political views. The 'new natural science' of bodies in motion, according to the traditional interpretation of influence, deeply infiltrates Hobbes's understanding of human life, and thereby influences his political philosophy. The '"root-paradigm" of inertial motion', Lisa Sarasohn says, 'analogically penetrated and transformed his [i.e., Hobbes's] understanding of both psychological behavior and political activity, and gave his social theories the status of cosmological realities'.[20] Hobbes, according to C. B. Macpherson, grounds his moral and political philosophy on the 'scientific hypothesis' that the 'motion of individual human beings could be reduced to the effects of a mechanical apparatus consisting of sense organs, nerves, muscles, imagination, memory and reason, which apparatus moved in response to the impact (or imagined impact) of external bodies on it'.[21] According to Spragens, 'Hobbes's fundamental psychological model is a human equivalent of the law of inertia'.[22] In this case, Hobbes applies one of Galileo's laws of motion to the internal motions of human beings. Michael Verdon believes the 'most appropriate model to use in the effort to find a systematic unity between Hobbes's physics and political philosophy is an atomistic version of Cartesian cosmology'.[23]

In the second case, Hobbes employs a resolutive-compositive methodology in his 'science of politics' to resolve the common-wealth and then reconstruct it. In this case the influence of geometry is apparent insofar as Hobbes carefully lays out axioms of human nature and then deduces a variety of political consequences. Adherents of the traditional interpretation correctly point out that Hobbes's natural philosophy influences his political philosophy in its application of a philosophical methodology to the political body. In this case, the commonwealth is resolved into its fundamental parts, which in turn are resolved into their parts. Such a resolution, according to this interpretation, stops at the primary principles of natural philosophy, which serve as the foundation for a synthetic or Euclidean-like demonstration of political conclusions. This view is dominant in Hobbes scholarship. In the words of David Gauthier, for example, Hobbes 'seeks to construct a unified science, proceeding from a study of body in general to a study of that particular body, man, and then to a study of man-made artificial bodies'.[24] C. B. Macpherson likewise claims Hobbes's political philosophy involves a *scientific* attempt to derive political conclusions on the basis of principles of human nature. In Macpherson's opinion, the first part of *Leviathan*, 'Of Man', simply lays out the primary principles of human behaviour that are used to derive psychological and political conclusions. John Watkins offers a clear expression of the political intentions behind Hobbes's appeal to geometry:

Hobbes learnt that a proposition whose truth by no means leaps to the eye or which is even counter-intuitive, may nevertheless be found to follow, by a chain of deductions, from propositions which seem obviously true. In proving Pythagoras's startling theorem, Euclid only invites us to attend to logical consequences of propositions which we 'already knew' in the sense that, although we may have been unaware of them, we were bound to assent to them if they were presented to us ... To do this became Hobbes's aim in his civil philosophy.[25]

All of these scholars accept that Hobbes's political philosophy is a deductive argument, similar to that found in geometry, founded on primary principles. While scholars disagree whether the primary principles of political philosophy are ultimately derived from a resolution to the fundamental principles of natural philosophy or are empirical principles concerning human nature, it is commonly accepted that Hobbes's political philosophy is oriented around a geometric procedure.

2.4 The Influence at Work: *Leviathan*

A brief glance at the main political argument of *Leviathan* reveals the general accuracy of the traditional interpretation of influence. The resolutive-compostive method provides a blueprint for the general structure of the treatise. Hobbes, according to this method, begins by resolving the commonwealth into its constitutive parts, i.e., humans, and then reconstructs the commonwealth through composition. In the early chapters of *Leviathan*, Hobbes presents his view of human nature or, more specifically, his view of humans as natural bodies. After this treatment, Hobbes reconstitutes the commonwealth by 'joining' individuals in a state of nature, from which the commonwealth eventually emerges. Once the commonwealth is created, Hobbes deduces a number of principles that are necessary for its maintenance and preservation. Throughout the whole reconstruction, Hobbes defines axioms, draws inferences and attempts to prove his political conclusions according to a geometrical model of proof.[26] In addition to the methodological influence of natural philosophy, the influence of Hobbes's 'science of motion' is revealed in his discussion of human nature, where human behaviour is described in terms of natural 'motions'. I will now take a closer look at the main argument of *Leviathan* to reveal more specifically the influence of natural philosophy and to provide a context for future discussion.[27]

2.4.a Hobbes's Philosophy of Mind and Psychology

The early chapters of *Leviathan* give us an insight into what may be called Hobbes's 'philosophy of mind' and his 'psychology'. Following other scholars, I refer to Hobbes's account of mental phenomena, e.g., sensation and imagination, as his 'philosophy of mind'. Hobbes's 'psychology' is a slightly broader term used to refer to his description of human behaviour in general and its causes.[28] In *De Corpore*, the philosophy of mind and psychology are parts of physics and comprise what Hobbes calls 'moral philosophy' (*Co* 6.72). In an important way, moral philosophy is the transition point from Hobbes's natural philosophy to his political philosophy. 'After physics,' Hobbes says, 'we must come to *moral philosophy*; in which we are to consider the motions of the mind, namely, *appetite, aversion, love, benevolence, hope, fear, anger, emulation*, &c.; what causes they have, and of what they be the causes' (*Co* 6.72). Moral philosophy is a part of physics because mental motions 'have their causes in sense and imagination, which are the subject of *physical contemplation*' (*Co* 6.73). On the other hand, moral philosophy is the starting point for Hobbes's political philosophy in the sense that it prepares the groundwork for his political conclusions. This is supported by the fact that *Leviathan*, Hobbes's most important political treatise, begins with an investigation of the 'motions of the human mind'.

The influence of the science of motion immediately appears when one looks at the sections in *Leviathan* that present Hobbes's philosophy of mind.[29] In the first chapter, Hobbes reveals his adherence to a mechanistic and materialist philosophy of mind when he claims that sensation is caused 'by the pressure, that is, by the motion, of externall things upon our Eyes, Ears, and other organs' (*L* 1.86).[30] Motions of external objects, he says, create a variety of 'fancies', or sensations, in the mind of the perceiver. Such motions linger in the mind and thereby generate the 'fancies of imagination', which are 'nothing but decaying sense' (*L* 2.88). The motions of sense and imagination, Hobbes continues, provide the 'first internall beginning of all Voluntary Motion' (*L* 6.118). External objects create motions in the mind, which themselves cause 'small beginnings of Motion, within the body of man, before they appear in walking, speaking, striking, and other visible actions, [which] are commonly called Endeavours' (*L* 6.119). Endeavours are divided into two types: appetites and aversions. An appetite is an endeavour that causes an individual to desire a particular object, such as hunger causes an individual to desire food. An aversion, on the other hand, causes one to avoid the object under consideration. Deliberation is the process of weighing appetites and aversions to determine what act, given the circumstances, will achieve the most good for the individual concerned (*L* 6.127). The weighing, however, is not really a matter of choice so much as it is the result of a mechanical process. Hobbes defines the will as the 'last Appetite, or Aversion, immediately adhering to the action, or to the omission thereof' (*L* 6.127). 'Appetites and Aversions, Hopes and Fears, concerning one and the same thing,' Hobbes says, 'arise alternately; and divers good and evil consequences of the doing, or omitting the thing propounded, come successively into view' (*L* 6.127). The final endeavour in this process is the cause of human action.

Hobbes's mechanistic and materialist account of voluntary motion leads to a pessimistic psychology, according to which the vast majority of people seek to attain the good, which is defined as 'whatsover is the object of any man's Appetite or Desire' (*L* 6.120).[31] Since the 'constitution of a man's Body is in constant mutation', Hobbes points out, 'it is impossible that all the same things should always cause in him the same appetites and aversions' (*L* 6.120). In addition, since each individual has different desires, Hobbes infers that all people do not consent in the 'Desire of almost anyone and the same good' (*L* 6.120). Hobbes advocates a subjective notion of the good here, according to which 'these words of Good, Evill, and Contemptible are ever used with relation to the person that useth them: There being nothing simply and absolutely so' (L 6.120). The good, in other words, is a purely descriptive term determined by the appetites of individuals. Hobbes believes, however, that almost everyone would agree that self-preservation is good and death is evil: 'For every man is desirous of what is good for him, and shuns what is evil, but chiefly the chiefest of natural evils, which is death' (*Ci* 1.115). The means by which individuals obtain their own good is power. The 'Power of a Man', Hobbes says, 'is his present means, to obtain some future apparent Good' (*L* 10.151). Since individuals are subject to a constant stream of appetites and aversions, Hobbes puts 'for a generall inclination of all mankind, a perpetual and restlesse desire of Power after power, that ceaseth only in Death' (*L* 11.161).

From the very start of *Leviathan*, then, the influence of natural philosophy on the political argument is apparent. Methodologically, Hobbes begins with an analysis of the 'parts' of the commonwealth, i.e. humans. Following a geometric model, he provides definitions of various mental phenomena and then draws a number of conclusions. In the process, he relies upon the mechanistic and materialistic principles of the new 'science of motion'. These foundational principles, as we shall see, ultimately influence many aspects of Hobbes's political philosophy.

2.4.b The State of Nature

Hobbes's psychological observations in the early chapters of *Leviathan* concern human individuals, not members of a community. As part of the 'reconstruction' of the commonwealth, Hobbes joins individuals together in a 'state of nature', a state prior to the formation of the commonwealth.[32] The first thing to recognize about the 'natural condition of mankind' is the relative equality of individuals within it. Although some humans are 'manifestly stronger in body' or 'of quicker mind', Hobbes claims that 'when all is reckoned together, the difference between man and man is not so considerable' that the 'weakest has strength to kill the strongest' (*L* 13.183). Equality, for Hobbes, is based upon the equal ability to kill or conquer others. In addition, Hobbes believes human conceit of one's own mental abilities reveals the equality of natural wit. Since most people hold their own wisdom to be greater than the wisdom of others, this 'proveth rather that men are in that point equal, than unequal' (*L* 13.184). After establishing the equal ability to kill, Hobbes explains how equality leads to conflict. In the first case, from the 'equality of ability, ariseth an equality of hope in the attaining of our ends' such that if two people desire the same thing that cannot be attained by both, they will 'become enemies' (*L* 13.184). To acquire desired objects, each person tries to 'destroy or subdue' the other (*L* 13.184). Faced with the threat of an enemy, Hobbes claims, it is reasonable to defend oneself through anticipatory violence. Through preemptory attacks on enemies, people are better equipped to conserve their own lives. The best offence, to use a sports analogy, is the best defence. And finally, Hobbes believes the desire to achieve glory, which is a characteristic of human nature, leads to conflict: 'For every man looketh that his companion should value him at the same rate he sets upon himself' (*L* 13.185). Thus, in the state of nature, there are three causes of conflict: competition, distrust and the desire for glory.

The natural condition of mankind, then, is a state of war in which life is 'solitary, poor, nasty, brutish, and short' (*L* 13.186). In such a state, Hobbes contends that each individual has a natural right to 'use his own power, as he will himselfe, for the preservation of his own Life; and consequently, of doing any thing, which in his own Judgement and Reason, he shall conceive to be the aptest means thereunto' (*L* 14.189). Individuals, in other words, are not constrained in the state of nature by any moral or legal obligations. In the state of nature 'nothing can be Unjust' since the 'notions of Right and Wrong, Justice and Injustice have there no place' (*L* 13.188). Human liberty is simply the 'absence of externall Impediments' and is not limited by any moral or legal notions. Because the state of nature is a state of war, individuals must seek peace if they wish to satisfy their egoistic desires, including the natural desire for self-preservation. For this reason, Hobbes claims, the 'Passions that encline men to Peace, are Feare of Death; Desire of such things as are necessary for commodious living; and a hope by their industry to attain them. And Reason suggesteth convenient Articles of Peace, upon which men may be drawn to agreement' (*L* 13.188). These 'articles of agreement', or 'laws of nature', are the means by which individuals escape the horrors of the state of nature.

2.4.c Laws of Nature

The geometric model of derivation is nowhere more apparent in Hobbes's political philosophy as it is in his treatment of the laws of nature. Definitions are provided and a series of conclusions are drawn in rapid fashion and there is a deep logical consistency to it all. A law of nature, Hobbes says, is a 'Precept, or generall Rule, found out by Reason, by which a man is forbidden to do, that, which is destructive of his life, or taketh away the means of preserving the same' (*L* 14.189). The first law of nature is that 'every man, ought to endeavor peace, as far as he has hope of obtaining it; and when he cannot obtain it, that he may seek, and use, all helps, and advantages of war' (*L* 14.190). The first part of this law, which is called the 'fundamental law of nature', directs individuals toward the satisfaction of their most dominant natural desire for self-preservation. Yet, in some cases, endeavouring for peace does not lead to self-preservation. Since peaceful coexistence requires reciprocity, if only one person seeks peace, it is unlikely it will be established. Thus, if others are not interested in settling a conflict, according to Hobbes, it is necessary to resort to the 'helps of war' to ensure one's survival. The second part of the first law of nature is called the 'sum of the right of nature' since the use of war is permitted by natural right.

From the fundamental law of nature, Hobbes deduces the remaining laws of nature. According to the second law of nature, because the retaining of natural right often keeps individuals in a state of war, peace requires that individuals renounce or transfer this right.

> From this Fundamental Law of Nature, by which men are commanded to endeavour peace, is derived this second law; That a man be willing, when others are so too, as farre- forth, as for peace, and defence of himselfe he shall think it necessary, to lay down this right to all things; and be contented with so much liberty against other men, as he would allow other men against himselfe. For as long as every man holdeth this Right, of doing anything he liketh; so long are all men in the condition of Warre. (*L* 14.190)

To put it simply, the natural right to all things is laid down either by transferring the right to a specific recipient or by renouncing the right entirely. To escape the hostile state of nature, Hobbes claims, individuals must create a common power by a mutual transferring of right.

> The only way to erect such a Common Power, as may be able to defend themselves from the invasion of foreigners, and the

injuries of one another, and thereby to secure them in such sort, as that by their own industrie, and by the fruits of the Earth, they may nourish themselves and live contentedly; is to conferre all their power and strength upon one Man, or Assembly of men, that may reduce all their Wills, by a plurality of voices, unto one Will. (*L* 17.227)

The transfer of the right to a common power is 'made by a covenant of every man with every man, in such manner, as if every man should say to every man, *I Authorise and give up my Right of Governing my selfe, to this man, or to this assembly of men*' (*L* 17.227). Yet, since the object of one's voluntary actions is some good to oneself, 'there be some rights, which no man can be understood by any words, or other signes, to have abandoned or transferred' (*L* 14.192). The purpose of establishing a common power is to escape from the condition of war, a condition that seriously threatens each person's conservation. Thus, a person cannot give up the natural right to self-preservation or to the means of self-preservation. By the second law of nature, then, 'we are obliged to transferre to another, such Rights, as being retained, hinder the Peace of Mankind' (*L* 15.201). This leads to the third law of nature that 'men perform their covenants made' (*L* 15.201). For a common power to perform the task for which it was erected, it is necessary that the covenanters follow through on their mutual agreement.

In *Leviathan*, Hobbes deduces 16 more laws of nature, all of which aim at maintaining the state of peace established by the erection of a common power. The fourth law of nature, for example, requires individuals to express gratitude for benefits received. If such gratitude is not expressed, escape from the state of war is not possible.

For no man giveth, but with intention of some Good to himselfe; because gift is Voluntary; and of all Voluntary Acts, the object is to every man his own Good; of which if men see they shall be frustrated, there will be no beginning of benevolence or trust; nor consequently of mutual help; nor of reconciliation of one man to another; and therefore they are to remain still in the condition of War; which is contrary to the first and Fundamental Law of Nature. (*L* 15.209)

Similarly, the other laws of nature are deduced from the fundamental law of nature commanding individuals to seek peace. At the end of his deduction of the laws of nature, Hobbes says 'these are the laws of nature, dictating peace, for a means of conservation of men in multitudes' (*L* 15.214).[33]

2.4.d The Sovereign Power

Peace, then, is made possible through the institution of a sovereign power. As we have seen, Hobbes claims the sovereign power may reside in 'one man or an assembly of men', so that a particular form of government is not required to maintain the peace. It is necessary, however, for the sovereign power to possess certain rights if it is to fulfill the task for which it was established. In a manner similar to the deduction of the laws of nature, Hobbes derives the 'rights and faculties' of the sovereign power (*L* 18.229). In the derivation of the rights of the sovereign power, Hobbes reveals those rights that are necessary for the maintenance of the peace. For example, the sovereign power has the right not to be dissolved by its subjects: 'they that are subjects to a monarch, cannot without his leave cast off monarchy, and return to a disunited multitude' (*L* 18.229).[34] Hobbes derives 11 other rights, all of which are 'incommunicable and inseparable' such that if 'any one of the said rights [are granted away], we shall presently see, that the holding of all the rest, will produce no effect, in the conservation of Peace and Justice, the end for which all Common-wealths are instituted' (*L* 18.236). The rights, briefly put, entail a defence of political absolutism. According to the basic tenets of Hobbes's political absolutism, the sovereign power enacts and enforces all laws, determines when to make war and peace, controls the military, judges all doctrines and opinions, decides all controversies between citizens, chooses its own counsellors and ministers, and cannot be legitimately resisted, except in rare instances.

For the present purposes, two aspects of Hobbes's political absolutism are important to emphasize. In the first case, Hobbes clearly states that the maintenance of civil order requires a civil sovereign with a coercive power to punish transgressors of the law. 'Consent', Hobbes says, 'is not sufficient security for their common peace, without the erection of some common power, by the fear whereof they may be compelled both to keep the peace amongst themselves, and to join their strengths together against a common enemy' (*El* 19.103). In *De Cive*, Hobbes similarly claims it is not enough 'to obtain this security, that every one of those who are not growing up in a city do covenant with the rest, either by words or by writing, not to steal, not to kill, and to observe the like laws' (*Ci* 6.176). It is not enough precisely because the 'pravity of the human disposition' is such that humans are likely to follow laws only if it suits their interests (*Ci* 6.176). 'We must therefore provide for our security', Hobbes says, 'not by compacts, but by punishment' (*Ci* 6.176). This view is echoed in *Leviathan*, where Hobbes claims 'it is no wonder if there be somewhat else required (besides Covenant) to make their Agreement constant and lasting; which is a Common Power, to keep them in awe, and to direct their actions to the Common Benefit' (*L* 17.226–7). With this power in hand, the sovereign may coerce citizens into lawful obedience.

In the second case, Hobbes's political absolutism includes the notion that the sovereign is the final arbiter on all matters ethical, religious and political. One of the 'diseases of a commonwealth,' Hobbes says, is the opinion that 'every private man is Judge of Good and Evill actions' (*L* 29.365). In the state of nature, as we have seen, individuals possess the natural right to determine what is good for themselves, i.e., what is necessary for their own conservation and comfort. As long as individuals make such determinations, Hobbes believes, there will be a state of war. For this reason, the sovereign must determine all doctrines and opinions in the commonwealth: 'It belongeth therefore to him that hath sovereign power, to be Judge, or constitute all Judges of Opinions and Doctrines, as a thing necessary to peace, thereby to prevent Discord and Civill Warre' (*L* 18.233). In established commonwealths, Hobbes believes religious doctrines are often responsible for civil conflict, especially in those cases where God's law and the civil law seem to be in opposition: 'When therefore these two powers [i.e., spiritual and temporal] oppose one another, the commonwealth cannot be but in great danger of civil war and dissolution' (*L* 29.371). In some commonwealths this problem does not exist because the civil authority wields both powers. 'There was no such dilemma among the Jews', Hobbes says, because 'the interpreters [of the Old Testament] whereof were the priests, whose power was subordinate to the power of the king' (*El* 6.145). Hobbes's solution to the problem of conflicting spiritual and temporal powers is to place them both under the control of the civil sovereign. If the interpretation of holy texts is granted to the civil sovereign, Hobbes argues, then the possibility of conflicting duties will vanish: 'It may therefore be concluded, that the interpretation of all laws, as well sacred as secular ... depends on the authority of the city, that is to say, that man or counsel to whom the sovereign power is committed; and that whatsoever God commands, he commands by his voice' (*Ci* 15.305).

Another important aspect of Hobbes's view of sovereignty is his marked preference for a monarchical form of government. In Chapter 19 of *Leviathan*, Hobbes discusses the kinds of commonwealths and the advantages and disadvantages that accrue to each. It is the number of people who wield the sovereign power that ultimately determines the form of the commonwealth.

When the Representative is One man, then is the commonwealth a Monarchy; when an Assembly of All that will come together, then it is a Democracy, or Popular Common-wealth: when an Assembly of a Part only, then it is called an Aristocracy (*L* 19.239).

There are no other types of governments, Hobbes says, despite the fact that some historical writers claim there are three other types: *tyranny*, *oligarchy* and *anarchy* (*L* 19.240). These 'are not the names of other Forms of Government', Hobbes says, 'but of the same forms misliked' (*L* 19.240). Those who do not approve of monarchy, for example, call it a tyranny. Of the three forms of governments, Hobbes believes monarchy surpasses the others in its 'Aptitude to produce the Peace, and Security of the people' (*L* 19.241). Hobbes gives five reasons for this superiority. First, 'in a monarchy, the private interest is the same with the publique' (*L* 19.241). Since sovereign representatives are egoistic human beings, if private and public interests clash, they will choose to advance their own good. Thus, 'where the publique and private interests are most closely united, there is the publique most advanced' (*L* 19.241). In democracies and aristocracies, Hobbes says, the prosperity of the people does not advance the private interests of the leaders as much as 'perfidious advice, a treacherous action, or a Civill warre' does (*L* 19.242). The second reason for the superiority of monarchy is that a monarch, when seeking advice, receives 'counsell of whom, when, and where he pleaseth' (*L* 19.242). When a sovereign assembly requires counsel, on the other hand, the meetings include people who are 'more versed in the acquisition of Wealth than of Knowledge' and who are wont to 'give their advice in long discourses, which may, and do commonly excite men to action, but not govern them in it' (*L* 19.243). Third, a monarch, when making a decision, is 'subject to no other Inconstancy, than that of Human Nature' (*L* 19.242). When resolutions are made in an assembly, the sheer number of people increases the risk of conflict since the desires of individuals are many. The decisions of a monarch, then, will be uniform and constant, providing added stability to government. Fourth, a sovereign 'cannot disagree with himself out of envy, or interest' (*L* 19.243). An assembly, on the other hand, is more likely to have a conflict of interest between its members. This conflict, according to Hobbes, may reach 'such a height, as may produce Civil Warre' (*L* 19.243). Finally, in a monarchy, only one person is subject to the desire to advance the interests of 'flatterers' or 'favourites' at the expense of the public interest. An increase in the number of people wielding sovereign power, Hobbes believes, will increase the number of flatterers and favourites, thereby increasing the chances of harm to the public interest (*L* 19.243).[35]

2.5 Conclusion

The brief summary of Hobbes's political argument of *Leviathan* has provided a context for the remaining chapters, wherein I present and defend the thesis of a political influence in Hobbes's natural philosophy. In this chapter, I have described the traditional interpretation of influence, an interpretation that is generally correct. Yet, it is incomplete and sometimes distorts the real picture. The problem with the traditional interpretation, as I see it, is that it either fails to recognize the political influence operative in Hobbes's natural philosophy or, in cases where a political influence is recognized, it considers natural philosophy simply as a scientific or logical basis for the political argument. The first type of failure, for example, is exhibited in Edwin Curley's assertion that *Leviathan* begins with 'topics apparently far removed from the subject of political obedience: the nature of thought, language, and science'.[36] In this case, the interpreter is blind to the political significance of these topics. Many scholars, however, note the political importance of Hobbes's natural philosophy, but only insofar as it is 'preliminary' to the main political argument. F. S. McNeilly, for example, claims the 'earlier chapters both of *The Elements of Law* and of *Leviathan*, in which Hobbes discusses language and method and gives a brief account of sense and imagination, are only preparatory to the chief arguments'.[37] Similarly, M. M. Goldsmith states that an 'examination of Hobbes's natural philosophy should provide us with an example of a Hobbesian science and with the principles that were the foundation of his political philosophy'.[38] Hobbes's natural philosophy, in other words, is politically important because it provides the foundational principles of political philosophy. The 'way in which Hobbes constructs the state from the passions and powers of its members (especially in the first part of *Leviathan)*', Machiel Karskens says, 'can be deduced from the methodological principles of his theory of science'.[39] The first part of *Leviathan*, wherein Hobbes presents his natural and moral philosophy, according to this view, is politically relevant because it provides the principles for the political argument. In the following chapters, I will explain why such a view is philosophically inadequate to a certain extent. Hobbes's natural philosophy, I hope to show, contains many elements that are packed with political significance, elements that are not simply preparatory to the political argument. Such significance strongly suggests, I will argue, that Hobbes's political ideas influence his natural philosophy.

Notes

1. I should emphasize at this point that the 'traditional interpretation of influence' does not refer to any specific philosophical interpretation of Hobbes, so much as it represents the fact that scholars, for the most part, have not explored the notion of a political influence on Hobbes's natural philosophy.
2. Before I offer a summary of Hobbes's philosophy, however, a word of caution is in order. A summary of any philosophical corpus is necessarily incomplete, selective and guided by the interpreter's concerns. In the final analysis, there really is no traditional and standard interpretation of Hobbes's entire philosophy, insofar as any summary would not be free of controversy. Scholars, as might be expected, disagree about many important issues in Hobbes's philosophy from start to finish. Thus, when I present a summary of his ideas, I will, by necessity, choose sides in

important debates. In cases where such debates exist, I will indicate this in the notes. With these cautionary remarks in place, then, I would like to emphasize that the goal of the following summary is to present those philosophical ideas that are important for the task of explicating the traditional interpretation of influence.

3. See Martinich, A. P. (1999), *Hobbes: A Biography*. Cambridge: Cambridge University Press, pp. 89–90.

4. See Tonnies, F., 'Introduction to *Elements of Law*' in *El* xii.

5. Lynch, W. T. (1991), 'Politics in Hobbes's Mechanics: The social as Enabling', *Studies in the History of the Philosophy of Science*, 22 (2), 305.

6. Ibid., p. 307.

7. Ibid., p. 306.

8. See Tuck, R. (1988), 'Hobbes and Descartes', in G. A. J. Rogers and A. Ryan (eds), *Perspectives on Thomas Hobbes*. Oxford: Clarendon Press, pp. 43–61.

9. See Martinich, *Hobbes*, p. 102.

10. The description of motion caused from a distance in the 'Short Tract' also combines a mechanistic view with Aristotelian elements: 'Every Agent that worketh on a distant Patient, touching it, either by the Medium, or by somewhat issueing from it self, which thing so issueing lett be call'd Species' (*ST* 2.197). The combination of mechanistic and Aristotelian elements is continued in the author's account of human motions: 'The Animal spirits are moved by the Species of Externall objects, immediately or mediately' (*ST* 3.205). This conclusion reveals the mechanistic view that human action, which is initiated by the 'animal spirits', is ultimately caused by the emotions of external objects. At the same time, however, it also reveals a commitment to an Aristotelian 'species' that emanates from the Agent continually (*ST* 2.199). Despite these Aristotelian remnants, the 'Short Tract' provides us with a rudimentary version of mechanism.

11. The exact nature of Hobbes's method, and if there is just one method, is a matter of scholarly debate. The standard view, held by John Watkins, C. B. Macpherson and David Gauthier, among others, is that Hobbes's method is basically inherited from Galileo's natural science. See Watkins, J. (1965), *Hobbes's System of Ideas*. London: Hutchinson & Co.; Macpherson, C. B. (1968), 'Introduction to *Leviathan*', in Hobbes, T., *Leviathan*. C. B. Macpherson (ed.). Harmondsworth: Penguin; Gauthier, D. (1969), *The Logic of Leviathan: The Moral and Political Theory of Thomas Hobbes*. Oxford: Clarendon Press. William Sacksteder, however, claims that Hobbes employs a distinct philosophical method in each branch of

philosophy, although there are commonalities in the distinct methods. See Sacksteder, W. (1992), 'Three Diverse Sciences in Hobbes: First Philosophy, Geometry, and Physics', *Review of Metaphysics*, 45, 739–72 and (1980), 'Hobbes: The Art of Geometricians', *Journal of the History of Philosophy*, 18, 131–46.

12. In *Leviathan*, Hobbes defines power as the 'present means to obtain some future apparent good' (*L* 10.150).

13. I will discuss Hobbes's philosophy of language in Chapter 5.

14. Chapter 5 will address Hobbes's theory of truth. It should be noted here that Hobbes, whether he is consistent or not, explicitly states his commitment to a conventional view of truth, at least with regard to the primary principles of geometry.

15. For different views on demonstration in Hobbes see: Hanson, D. (1990), 'The Meaning of "Demonstration" in Hobbes's Science', *History of Political Thought*, 11, 587–626; Sacksteder, 'Hobbes: The Art of Geometricians'; Talaska, R. (1988), 'Analytic and Synthetic Method According to Hobbes', *Journal of the History of Philosophy*, 26, 207–37. According to Hanson, scholars too often ascribe an anachronistic notion of demonstration to Hobbes, failing to see that Hobbes's demonstration is supposed to find proofs, not discover new truths. Sacksteder, on the other hand, criticizes Hobbes scholars for overlooking the specific methodology of geometry and thereby missing the peculiar nature of geometric demonstration. Talaska claims Hobbes's method does provide a means of discovering new truths.

16. For an interesting interpretation of the importance of the science of motion to Hobbes's philosophy as a whole, see Spragens, T. (1973), *The Politics of Motion: The World of Thomas Hobbes: Its Basis and Its Genesis*. Lexington, KY: University of Kentucky Press. In this book, Spragens advances the traditional interpretation of influence when he claims that Galileo's science of motion was adopted by Hobbes as a paradigm, which was then applied to an Aristotelian framework.

17. In the first section of the present chapter, I discussed the contrast between composition and resolution in terms of wholes and parts; composition involves constructing wholes from parts, while resolution involves breaking up wholes into their parts. Despite the change in terminology, Hobbes's physics is still concerned with taking apart wholes in order to discover their constituent parts. An investigation into the physical world, as Hobbes claims, must begin with how natural bodies appear to us. In order to discover the causes of such appearances, one might say that

Hobbes resolves the whole event into the perceiver and the external world. Hobbes then proceeds to resolve each of these in turn.

18. Hobbes's theory of sensation will be fully addressed in Chapter 4.

19. According to what I am calling the traditional interpretation of influence, Hobbes's natural philosophy controls and guides his political philosophy in a variety of ways. Adherents of the traditional interpretation do not necessarily agree on the manner in which natural philosophy has influenced Hobbes. In fact, the only thing shared in common is the failure to recognize the political influence on Hobbes's natural philosophy. I characterize the traditional interpretation in such a negative manner to account for the fact that a fair number of interpreters deny the systematic nature of Hobbes's philosophy. Thus, the non-systematic interpreters often neglect to mention the obvious influence of Hobbes's natural philosophy on his political philosophy, not to mention the converse influence, since these scholars are inclined to focus on the independent nature of the philosophical branches.

20. Sarasohn, L. T. (1985), 'Motion and Morality: Peirre Gassendi, Thomas Hobbes, and the Mechanical World-View', *Journal of the History of Ideas*, 46, 363.

21. Macpherson, 'Introduction to *Leviathan*', pp. 28–9.

22. Spragens, *The Politics of Motion*, p. 189.

23. Verdon, M. (1982), 'On the Laws of Physical and Human Nature: Hobbes's Physical and Social Cosmologies', *Journal of the History of Ideas*, 43, 656.

24. Gauthier, D. (1969), *The Logic of Leviathan: The Moral and Political Theory of Thomas Hobbes*. Oxford: Clarendon Press, p. 2.

25. Watkins, *Hobbes's System*, p. 13.

26. Macpherson, 'Introduction to *Leviathan*', p. 29.

27. The summary focuses on a specific argument, the one normally given by traditional interpreters.

28. See, for example, Barnouw, J. (1989), 'Hobbes's Psychology of Thought: Endeavours, Purpose and Curiousity', *History of European Ideas*, 10, 519–45; Lott, T. (1982), 'Hobbes's Mechanistic Psychology', in J. G. van der Bend (ed.), *Thomas Hobbes: His View of Man*. Amsterdam: Rodopi B.V., pp. 63–75.

29. In one sense, it seems obvious that Hobbes's natural philosophy influences his moral philosophy since the latter is a branch of the former. Hobbes's first treatment of human nature in *De Corpore*, for instance, is the chapter on 'Sense and Animal Motion', which is included in Part IV of the book,

i.e., the part that contains Hobbes's physics. What is important to recognize is how Hobbes's philosophy of mind, and his psychology, is ultimately shaped by his scientific view of motion and how this guides the political argument in *Leviathan*.

30. I will discuss Hobbes's philosophy of mind in Chapter 4. It should be noted here, however, that William Sacksteder believes it is a 'mis-interpretation' to say Hobbes has a mechanistic and materialist philosophy of mind. This is due to his opinion that the mechanistic-materialist interpretation makes it almost 'impossible to speak about mind within his [Hobbes's] scheme'. Hobbes, in Sacksteder's opinion, does provide 'sophisticated ways for speaking about mind'. See Sacksteder, W. (1979), 'Speaking About Mind: *Endeavour* in Hobbes', *The Philosophical Forum*, 11, 65.

31. Scholars disagree as to whether Hobbes is a psychological pessimist or a psychological egoist. Bernard Gert argues that Hobbes is best viewed as an adherent of psychological pessimism, which states that *most* people are driven by the desire to satisfy their own interests. Egoism simply universalizes this claim. See Gert, B. (1965a) 'Hobbes and Psychological Egoism', *Journal of the History of Ideas*, 28, 503–20 and (1965b), 'Hobbes, Mechanism, and Egoism', *Philosophical Quarterly*, 15, 341–9. Tommy Lott provides a critique of Gert's position in Lott, T. (1974), 'Motivation and Egoism in Hobbes', *Kinesis*, 6, 112–25.

32. The details of Hobbes's description of the state of nature vary in *Elements of Law*, *De Cive* and *Leviathan*. For a detailed account of these differences see Hinnant, C. (1977), *Thomas Hobbes*. Boston, MA: Twayne Publishers; McNeilly, F. S. (1968), *The Anatomy of Leviathan*. London: St Martin's Press. My summary is primarily based on *Leviathan*.

33. My summary has intentionally bypassed what might be the most controversial issue in Hobbes scholarship, namely, whether the laws of nature constitute a genuine moral theory. As might be expected, Hobbes's moral theory, if he has one, is interpreted in different ways. He is variously considered as a moral contractarian, a divine-command theorist, and as a virtue ethicist. According to the moral contractarian interpretation, morality is artificially created in order to satisfy human desires, especially the desire for self-preservation. See, for example, Gauthier, *The Logic of Leviathan*. Hobbes's laws of nature could also be interpreted as divine commands whose moral force has theological underpinnings. According to this interpretation, the laws of nature have both a prudential and a moral character. As a matter of fact, following the laws of nature results in

benefits for the individual, but the reason one should follow them is because God commands them. The best defence of this position is found in Warrender, H. (1957), *The Political Philosophy of Hobbes: His Theory of Obligation*. Oxford: Clarendon Press. Hobbes's moral philosophy has recently been interpreted as an 'ethics of character rather than of action'. The laws of nature, according to this virtue ethicist position, is precisely a science of 'virtues and vices' in the sense that these terms refer to habits and dispositions. See Boonin-Vail, D. (1994), *Thomas Hobbes and the Sciences of Moral Virtue*. Cambridge: Cambridge University Press, p. 108.

34. Although Hobbes specifically refers to monarchy here, his point applies to all forms of sovereignty.

35. Hobbes provides a sixth consideration in which he discusses one of the inconveniences of monarchy, viz., the problems that arise when the sovereignty is granted to a child by the right of succession. In this case, Hobbes claims the problems are not attributable to monarchy specifically. Instead, the problems are basically identical to those in a democracy or aristocracy. See *L* 19.243.

36. Curley, E. (1994), 'Introduction to Hobbes's *Leviathan*', in E. Curley (ed.), *Leviathan*. Indianapolis, IN: Hackett Publishing, pp. viii–ix.

37. McNeilly, *The Anatomy of Leviathan*, p. 95.

38. Goldsmith, M. M. (1966), *Hobbes's Science of Politics*. New York: Columbia University Press, p. 14.

39. Karskens, M. (1982), 'Hobbes's Mechanistic Theory of Science, and its Role in his Anthropology', in J. G. van der Bend (ed.), *Thomas Hobbes: His View of Man*. Amsterdam: Rodopi B.V., p. 4.

3

Hobbes's Political Agenda

3.0 Introduction

In the previous chapter, I described the traditional interpretation of influence, according to which Hobbes's natural philosophy is politically relevant, if at all, insofar as it provides the theoretical grounding of his political argument. In contrast to the traditional interpretation, I intend to show that Hobbes's natural philosophy is not only relevant for his political ideas, but that these political ideas influence and guide Hobbes toward the adoption of certain 'strictly philosophical' views. As I pointed out in Section 1.1.c, Hobbes's 'political ideas' are comprised of both his political agenda, which refers to the practical political goals he was trying to accomplish, and his political philosophy, which refers to the theoretical goals of his political science. In Section 2.4, I outlined the main elements of Hobbes's political philosophy. In this chapter, I present the main goals of Hobbes's *political agenda*. In the process, I hope to show that the major aspects of Hobbes's political agenda remained quite consistent throughout his life. As might be expected, scholars disagree on what Hobbes was trying to accomplish by presenting his political philosophy to the world. Thus, I begin in Section 3.1 by presenting competing views of Hobbes's political solution. This presentation will reveal that a proper comprehension of Hobbes's agenda requires us to investigate his 'historical' works and not just the treatises of his political philosophy. In Sections 3.2 and 3.3, then, I use his historical writings to reveal the specific political opponents with whom Hobbes was concerned. Concluding remarks will be made in Section 3.4.

3.1 Hobbes's Political Solution: Competing Views

One of the obvious goals of Hobbes's political agenda is to provide a means for resolving the civil conflict tearing his country apart. Traditionally, scholars focus on Hobbes's account of the state of nature when trying to understand his solution to the problem of civil discord. According to the traditional view, Hobbes provides a 'coercive solution' whereby the sovereign maintains peace by the threat of punishment. A coercive solution is required because humans are naturally at war with each other unless there is a power to keep them in check. In contrast to this interpretation, some scholars argue that the coercive solution is not sufficient because the behaviour of many individuals, especially those who are driven by political or religious ideals, is not affected by the threat of punishment. According to this view, or what I will call the 'ideological solution' of civil disorder, the sovereign must control opinions to establish and maintain peace. Scholars who believe Hobbes's main goal is to provide an ideological solution to civil disorder criticize traditional interpreters for failing to correctly identify his analysis of the political problem. This failure is due, in part, to the overly narrow focus on Hobbes's philosophical works and, more specifically, on his account of the state of nature. What Hobbes considers the real political problem, it is argued, is best found in his historical writings.

According to S. A. Lloyd, most Hobbes scholars adhere to the coercive solution to the problem of civil disorder.[1] Hobbes's coercive solution, in the words of Lloyd, is 'to set up a coercively empowered sovereign that can, by threat of punishment, compel individuals to behave in a manner that does not threaten the security of their fellows'.[2] The coercive solution depends on the view that humans, in a state of nature, are motivated to achieve their own good, including the good of self-preservation. Since the natural state is a state of war, wherein self-preservation and the attainment of goods are constantly threatened, it is rational for individuals to establish a sovereign with sufficient power to make antisocial behaviour contrary to one's self-interests. Without such a sovereign power, humans will remain in a state of war. As Hobbes says, 'during that time men live without a common Power to keep them all in awe, they be in a condition which is called Warre' (*L* 13.185). The coercive solution, in other words, holds that the existence and the enforcement of law are the most important factors in the maintenance of order. Since most individuals tend to be driven by the desire to lead pleasurable or satisfying lives, the threat of punishment is often enough to make many potential criminals think twice about committing illegal acts. The sovereign power has 'so much Power and Strength conferred upon, that by terror thereof, he is inabled to forme the wills of them all, to Peace at home and mutual aid against their enemyes abroad' (*L* 17.227). In the words of Gregory Kavka, Hobbes's solution is to 'alter the payoffs':

> Hobbes proposes a plausible solution to the problem of individual and collective rationality: the creation of a power to impose sanctions that would alter the parties' payoffs so as to synchronize individual and collective rationality.[3]

Assuming that rational behaviour is identified with what is in one's own interests, the sovereign power uses the threat of punishment to make lawful and social behaviour beneficial to everyone.

The coercive solution faces a major problem insofar as the threat of punishment is not always sufficient to control people's opinions, and thereby their actions. As Lloyd argues, Hobbes implies 'there are forces other than considerations of rational self-interest capable of affecting human behavior'.[4] Hobbes says, for example, that 'most men would rather lose their lives than suffer slander' (*Ci* 3.142). He also claims that 'a son will rather die than live infamous and hated of all the world' (*Ci* 6.183). According to Lloyd, these passages entail that 'people are capable of forming, and acting on, transcendent interests. Of pursuing principles over preservation. Of exerting mind over matter.'[5] If it is the case that certain individuals are prepared to sacrifice their own lives for transcendent interests, then the threats of a sovereign power will have no effect. As Hobbes points out, people often hold 'seditious opinions' that lead them to disobey civil laws, even though the threat of punishment is attached to such disobedience. Thus, to maintain a state of peace, the sovereign power must be able to keep rebellious doctrines from spreading. Hobbes's solution, according to this view, is to unify *conflicting opinions*.

Scholars who believe Hobbes offers an ideological solution claim the historical writings have a 'logical' priority because they reveal the fundamental problem addressed in the political writings. Robert Kraynack, for example, claims that *Behemoth*, which is Hobbes's own history of the English Civil War written in 1668, is of primary importance for the interpretation of his political philosophy.[6] Kraynack criticizes the traditional view that *Behemoth* is of 'secondary importance' because it 'applies principles previously articulated in *Leviathan*'.[7] The traditional view is declared inadequate because it is 'based on an inference that fails to grasp the true relationship between Hobbes's histories and scientific treatises [on political philosophy]'.[8] The true relationship, according to Kraynack, is that the scientific political treatises attempt to solve the problem that is clearly revealed in the historical texts.

In *Behemoth*, Hobbes not only narrates the events of the civil war, but also tries to indicate their causes (*B* 220). The work begins with a simple question: how did King Charles I, being a 'man who wanted no virtue, either of body or mind', lose the sovereignty that he held 'by right of a descent continued above six hundred years' (*B* 166)? The initial response to this question is perfectly consistent with the traditional interpretation that claims civil conflict is caused by the lack of a coercive sovereign power. King Charles I, says Hobbes, could not keep control of the kingdom because he was deprived of the financial resources required to maintain a military. The ultimate cause of disorder, in other words, was the King's loss of coercive power, a force necessary for defence against foreign enemies and internal rebels. Upon further consideration, however, one discovers a more fundamental cause of conflict. The main reason behind the King's loss of power, one might say, was the fact that the 'people were corrupted' by 'seducers of divers sorts' to accept opinions and beliefs not conducive to social and political harmony (*B* 167). 'The actions of men', Hobbes says in *Leviathan*, 'proceed from their opinions, and in the well governing of opinions, consists the well governing of men's actions, in order to their peace and concord' (*L* 18.233). The sovereign power must not only have the power to punish lawbreakers, but also the ability to control people's opinions as a preventative measure against neglect of duty. For this reason, the sovereign power must 'judge, or constitute all judges of opinions and doctrines, as a thing necessary to peace, thereby to prevent discord and civill warre' (*L* 18.233).

Locating the source of civil disorder in the spread of seditious opinions, one could say the goal of Hobbes's political science is to put an end to what Kraynack refers to as 'doctrinal politics'.

> [T]heir corruption consisted in acquiring an artificial concern for general and abstract principles of right. In *Behemoth* corruption is the process by which people are indoctrinated by intellectual authorities (priests, scholars, and political demagogues) in the literal sense of being filled up with doctrines and turned into zealous partisans. As a result, the raising of armies depended not on monetary rewards or material incentives but on the control of opinions and doctrines. The central issue of *Behemoth*, therefore, is the question of who corrupted the people into becoming practitioners of doctrinal politics.[9]

The King lost his sovereignty, to put it simply, when he lost the control of the people's opinions. To maintain sovereign power, then, the sovereign must prevent the dissemination of seditious doctrines.

As we have seen, then, there are two ways to interpret Hobbes's solution for the problem of political upheaval. On the one hand, the ideological solution involves the neutralization of seditious and rebellious opinions through political indoctrination. On the other hand, the coercive solution is to establish a sovereign with enough power to compel citizens into obedience. The two interpretations, however, are not mutually exclusive, as is evidenced by Hobbes's discussion of 'those things that Weaken, or tend to the Dissolution of a Commonwealth' (*L* 29.363). The first item mentioned is that a king is 'sometimes content with less Power, than to the Peace, and Defence of the Commonwealth is necessarily required' (*L* 29.364). In the second case, Hobbes claims the 'Diseases of a Commonwealth ... proceed from the poyson of seditious doctrines' (*L* 29.365). These two facts are intricately linked such that a king with a large amount of coercive power is better able to control the ideas circulating within the commonwealth, e.g., by controlling the universities and the printing presses, and by threatening 'rebellious' individuals. And, vice versa, a king with the control of public opinion increases his coercive power and does not have to exercise it often. Yet, as has been pointed out, coercive power is not always sufficient to control the actions of every individual. The more that seditious doctrines spread, the more likely the sovereign's coercive power will become ineffective. Hobbes, by presenting a political philosophy in the form of a science, hopes to prove that his doctrine will lead to peace and security among warring factions.

> But in this time, that men call not only for Peace, but also for Truth, to offer such Doctrines as I think True, and that manifestly lead to Peace and Loyalty, to the consideration of those that are yet in deliberation, is no more, but to offer New Wine, to be put into New Cask, that both may be preserved together. (*L* Review 726)

Hobbes, in other words, presents a new kind of doctrine, which includes the notion of the necessity of a coercive sovereign power.[10] In the *Elements of Law*, Hobbes remarks, it 'would be an incomparable benefit to the commonwealth, if every man held the opinions concerning law and policy here delivered' (*El* Epistle xvi). The acceptance of Hobbes's science of politics is supposed to produce agreement not only in the realm of ideas, but also in the realm of practice. Since many conflicts arise because of contrasting opinions, agreement in theory will reduce the possibility of actual conflict.

The contrast between the ideological and the coercive solutions to the problem of civil disorder manifests an important point for the primary goal of this work. As previously mentioned, this chapter is concerned with revealing Hobbes's political agenda. As the adherents of the ideological interpretation have pointed out, the historical works are a good source for understanding what dangerous political ideas Hobbes is trying to counteract. Thus, in the following sections, I discuss Hobbes's historical works: the translation of Thucydides' *History of the Peloponnesian Wars* (1629), *Behemoth* (1678) and *A Dialogue between A Philosopher and A Student of the Common Laws* (1679).

3.2 Hobbes's Early Political Agenda

In 1629, at the age of 41, Hobbes witnessed the first publication of his career, or at least the first publication under his own name. The work was a translation of Thucydides' *History of the Peloponnesian Wars*. Hobbes's interest in translating classical works had begun at an early age. By the age of 14, he was adept enough in Latin and Greek to translate Euripides' *Medea* into Latin verse. His Latin skills were probably honed through the writing of essays on the classics and history in his twenties. It is possible that Hobbes may have seen some of his Latin essays anonymously published in 1620. In a collection of essays entitled *Horae Subsecivae*, there are three essays that scholars now attribute to Hobbes: 'Of Rome', 'A Discourse on the Beginning of Tacitus' and 'Of Laws'.[11] Another early work of Hobbes, *De Mirabilibus Pecci*, is a poem written to commemorate a trek through the Peak District in 1626. This work was eventually published in 1636. For the most part, this literature tells us more about Hobbes's early interests in classical humanism and history than about his political ideas. As Miriam Reik points out, if Hobbes 'had died before his forty-first year, he would probably be remembered as a rather minor representative of the last generation of Tudor humanists and translators who did so much to appropriate classical culture to the English language'.[12]

In this section, I focus on the translation of Thucydides' *History of the Peloponnesian Wars* as the primary source of information about Hobbes's early political agenda. An investigation into the circumstances surrounding the publication of the translation and into the translation itself reveals four important political ideas of Hobbes, ideas that are central not only to his political agenda, but also to his inchoate political philosophy: (1) political power functions most effectively when it is centralized, (2) monarchy is preferable to democracy, (3) civil disorder is frequently caused by demagogues who misuse speech, and (4) religion is a source of civil problems.

According to A. P. Martinich, it is safe to assume that Hobbes had begun to translate Thucydides' work by the middle of the 1620s, around the time that troubles between Charles I and Parliament had started to escalate.[13] It had been finished by 1628, the year in which Hobbes registered his translation with the Company of the Stationers in London. Although Hobbes may have started the work without any political intention in mind, which seems improbable given his political connections, it is likely that he considered its publication a political act because of its timing.[14] In 1626, Charles I assembled Parliament to raise funds for war efforts against Spain and France. At this point, war was openly declared against Spain and Charles I was amassing the largest entourage of forces since the war against Spain in 1588. In England, a Spanish war was unpopular for a number of reasons, including its negative effects on trade and the early losses suffered at Cadiz. Concurrently, tensions between England and France were on the rise. French maritime conflicts, for example, resulted in the enactment of embargoes, thereby adding more complications to international trade. In addition, tensions were increased by two other causes, namely, the French possession of English ships (which were originally on loan) and the religious differences between the nations (France was dominantly Catholic).

The Parliament of 1626 refused Charles' request for supply, thereby prompting him to raise funds through a forced loan. The forced loan not only created further tension between Charles I and Parliament, but it also raised a number of ideological issues with serious political implications. The Five Knights' Case, as the historian Conrad Russell points out, 'arose out of the Forced Loan, but soon acquired an importance in many people's minds which far transcended that of the Loan'.[15] The case began when five knights were imprisoned for their refusal to pay the loan. In response to a Habeas Corpus suit by the knights, the King's attorney was required to show in court the cause of their imprisonment. By raising the suit, the knights ostensibly hoped to challenge the legality of the forced loan in court, since it was expected that the royal attorney would cite their refusal to pay as the cause of their imprisonment. The attorney, however, claimed the knights were imprisoned '*per special mandatum domini reges*' (by special command of the king). Rather than being a test case on the legality of the loan, according to Russell, it 'became a test case on the King's prerogative power to imprison those who had offended him without showing any cause'.[16] The case, in other words, raised specifically political questions about the relationship between the King's prerogative and the law. The answers given to such questions would reveal serious ideological differences between King and Parliament. The 'King's overt claim to imprison on discretion', for example, 'threatened the centre of Coke's legal ideal: the freedom to live by settled and known rules of law'.[17]

The ideological debate concerning the King's prerogative power and its relationship to the law is thoroughly treated by Russell, so I will not repeat the account here. For the present purposes, we may summarize the debate by recounting statements made by the advocates of the opposing sides. In the 1628 Parliament, Sir Robert Phelips complained of the infringement on his liberties following from the King's right to imprison without cause:

> Nay, I can live though I pay excises and impositions for more than I do, but to have my liberty (which is the soul of my life) taken from me by power, and to be pent up in a gaol without remedy by law, and to be so adjudged (shall I perish in a gaol). O improvident ancestors! O unwise forefathers! to be so curious in providing for the quiet possession of our lands, and the liberties of Parliament, and to neglect our persons and bodies, and to let them lie in prison, and that, *durante beneplacito*, remediless. If this be law, what do we talk of our liberties?[18]

In a letter responding to the sentiments expressed by MPs such as Phelips, the King clearly asserted his conviction that his right to imprison was not limited by civil law:

> We still find it insisted on, that in no case whatsoever, though they should never so clearly concern matters of state and government, we or our Privy Council have power to commit a man without the cause shown, whereas it often happens that should the cause be shown the service itself would thereby be destroyed and defeated. And the cause alleged must be such as may be determined by our judges of our courts at Westminster in a legal and ordinary way of justice, whereas the causes may be such as those judges have no capacity of judicature nor rules of law to direct and guide their judgments in causes of that

transcendent nature ... Without overthrow of sovereignty we cannot suffer this power to be impeached. Notwithstanding to clear our conscience and just intentions, we publish that it is not in our heart, nor will we ever extend our regal power (lent unto us from God) beyond that just rule of moderation in any thing which shall be contrary to our laws and customs, wherein the safety of our peoples, shall be our only aim.[19]

Although the King tried to reassure his subjects by saying he would not use royal power inappropriately, he unequivocally declared that God granted him the right to act outside the law.

The King's insistence on the right to imprison outside the law sparked serious doubts as to whether he could be trusted to act in good faith. The King raised such doubts not only by his words and actions concerning extra-legal imprisonment, but also by amassing a large army of troops by the winter of 1627–8. As Russell shows us, what was so alarming about this situation was that if the King 'wished to set up an "arbitrary government," he had possible means of enforcing his will'.[20] In addition, the King's troops needed to be housed, and so the question of billeting became a further catalyst for escalating tensions. Once again, common law lawyers such as Coke, who believed the forced billeting of soldiers was contrary to the law, questioned the legality of the King's orders. The Petition of Right, presented in Parliament in 1628, sought to preserve the liberties of the subjects against the threatening actions of the King, such as forced loans, extra-legal imprisonment and the billeting of soldiers.[21]

In addition to politics, religion played a role in promoting troubles in England. Both Charles I and his predecessor were cognizant of the fact that religious leaders presented a genuine threat to their political authority. In 1633, the Exchequer court prohibited the 'feoffees for impropriations', which provided financial support to Puritan lecturers. According to historian Ann Hughes, the prohibition was established because 'Charles and his authoritarian associates feared a popular subversive attack from Puritans stilled up by factious lecturers'.[22] In a speech to the House of Lords nine years earlier, James I expressed his disdain for Puritan lectures because of the threat posed by them to his crown:

> I think it is all one to lay down my crown to the Pope as to a popular party of Puritans . . . I commend my Lord of Norwich for suppressing of popular lectures within his diocese. I mean such as are nowadays most frequented, being supplied and held up by such ministers as have not care of souls where they preached, for such must flatter and cog and claw the people and therefore I will never allow them.[23]

While historians have different opinions as to the extent to which Puritanism is responsible for the eventual outbreak of civil war, one thing is clear: religious differences were at least partially responsible for increasing political tensions in the 1620s.[24]

One of the major causes of concern for English Protestants during this time, including both traditional Anglicans and the more radical Puritans, was Charles' ardent support of Archbishop Laud, who was a sponsor of a number of Arminian policies. Such policies were inspired by the anti-Calvinist views of Dutch theologian Arminius, who claimed the elect could fall from God's grace through sin, thereby calling into question the Calvinist notion of predestination. English Protestants believed that the Arminians, since they employed many ritualistic and ceremonial practices in their religious observance, were very close to 'popery'. Such similarities to Roman Catholicism were a source of political concern for many Protestants. In the Parliament of 1628, Christopher Sherland expressed his worries about Arminianism: 'Why are Arminians that have sought the ruin of the Low Countries allowed here? They run in a string with the papists and flatter greatness to oppress the subject'.[25] According to Hughes, it was precisely the 'pressure of Arminianism, backed enthusiastically by

Charles I and his Archbishop William Laud, that turned hitherto conventional, conservative English Protestants into opponents of the crown'.[26] King Charles I, on the other hand, believed that Laud represented the traditional and orthodox position. In 1626, the King, according to a proclamation partially drafted by his archbishop, prohibited 'any new Opinions, not only contrary, but differing from the sound and orthodoxal grounds of the true religion, sincerely professed, and happily established in the Church of England'.[27] The debates spurred on by Charles' advocacy of Arminianism, Russell suggests, created a 'new intellectual link' between religion and politics, which became an explicit topic in the parliamentary debates of 1628:

> Here is a new intellectual link: the connection of the alteration of religion with the alteration of government. Those who wish to alter religion wish to alter government, in order to protect themselves from questioning: those who wish to alter government provoke quarrels with Parliaments by supporting those who would alter religion.[28]

Advocates on each side, as might be expected, believed their religious opponents were the reactionaries preaching new, and politically dangerous, doctrines.

This historical venture into the ideological conflicts between King Charles I and Parliament reveals that questions concerning the ultimate locus of political authority were at the forefront of English political consciousness in the years just prior to Hobbes's publication of his translation of Thucydides. For the 'first time in the 1620s', Russell claims, 'Parliamentary proceedings came to be dominated by a contest between King and the Commons about the nature and limits of supreme authority'.[29] In addition, Russell points out that manuscripts of Parliamentary speeches and debates brought such issues to the public at large. English citizens celebrated the passing of the Petition of Right with numerous bonfires.[30] If it is true, as Miriam Reik claims, that Hobbes 'was goaded into the publication of the *History* by the appearance of the Petition of Right in the previous year, finding in Thucydides an argument for the king', then it is necessary to take the historical context into account in interpreting Hobbes's political intentions for publishing his translation.[31] Hobbes himself supports the truth of Reik's claim when he states, in his autobiography, that Thucydides' history provided instruction useful for the defence of the King (*OL* xxxviii).

In the introduction to Thucydides' history, Hobbes claims the 'principal and proper work of history' is 'to instruct and enable men by the knowledge of their actions past, to bear themselves prudently and providently towards the future' (*T* vii). Hobbes confirms the instructive nature of the work when he claims that 'Thucydides' narration itself doth secretly instruct the reader' (*T* xii). But what specific lesson may be found in this ancient history according to Hobbes? If we assume that the publication was in response to the Petition of Right and that it was meant to provide a defence of King Charles, then we may infer that Hobbes wanted to counteract the politically dangerous opinions of the King's opponents. This inference is supported by the fact that Hobbes clearly states his preference of monarchy over democracy. According to Hobbes's autobiography, the goal of publishing *Thucydides* was to 'point out how inadequate democracy is, and how much wiser one man is than a multitude' (*OL* xxxviii). In his discussion of Thucydides' political beliefs, Hobbes clearly endorses the opinion that democracy poses many threats to political stability:

For his [Thucydides] opinion touching government of the state, it is manifest that he least of all liked democracy. And upon diverse occasions he noteth the emulation and the contention of the demagogues for reputation and glory of wit; with their crossing of each other's counsels, to the damage of the public; the inconsistency of the resolutions, caused by the diversity of ends and power of rhetoric in the orators; and the desperate actions undertaken upon the flattering advice of such as desired to attain, or to hold what they had attained, of authority and sway among the common people. (*T* xvi–xvii)

One finds in this passage Hobbes's early disdain of democracy and some of the motivations driving him to prefer monarchy.

One of the problems with democracy, according to the above passage, is the fact that the common people are easily swayed by the rhetorical power of demagogues, who seek the advancement of their own 'reputation and glory of wit'. Hobbes indicates that he admires Thucydides for not exploiting naturally given rhetorical abilities to play the role of the demagogue. Thucydides, Hobbes says, was 'sufficiently qualified to become a great demagogue and of great authority with the people', but 'he had no desire at all to meddle in the government' (*T* xvi). Hobbes points out that Thucydides was not one of the many 'flatterers' who drove the common people 'headlong into those actions that were to ruin them' (*T* xvi). Given the historical situation of English political life, it is likely that Hobbes uses 'demagogues' to refer to anyone who raises doubts about the *King's* authority through speeches and lectures. In addition, at this time, Hobbes was probably already aware of the dangerous effects of religious lecturers, as were Charles and James. In addition, given the many speeches in Parliament against the King, speeches that were frequently made public, it is likely that Hobbes believed common law lawyers, such as Coke, were attempting to encourage the people toward unlawful disobedience.

From Thucydides, Hobbes also learns the lesson that the misuse of language leads to dangerous consequences for the state. In the following passage from the *History*, one finds a theme that will become important for Hobbes in his works of political philosophy, that is, the political power of language.

War ... is a most violent master, and conformeth most men's passions to the present occasion ... The received value of names imposed for signification of things, was changed into arbitrary. For inconsiderate boldness, was counted true-hearted manliness; provident deliberation, a handsome fear; modesty, the cloak of cowardice; to be wise in everything, to be lazy in every thing ... He that did insidiate, if it took, was a wise man; but he that could smell out a trap laid, a more dangerous man than he. But he that had been so provident as not to need to do one or the other, was said to be a dissolver of society. In brief, he that could outstrip another in the doing of an evil act, or that could persuade another thereunto that never meant it, was commended. (*T* 348–9)

It may be inferred that one of the lessons Hobbes wants to communicate is, as Martinich puts it, that the 'rhetoric of the king's enemies was threatening the stability of the nation'.[32]

Thucydides also teaches the important lesson that religious dogmatism is politically dangerous. Hobbes suggests that Thucydides might have 'seen enough in the religion of these heathens, to make him think it vain and superstitious' (*T* xv). At one point in the *History*, as Hobbes notes, Thucydides 'taxeth Nicias for being too punctual in the observation of the ceremonies of their religion, when he overthrew himself and his army, and indeed the whole dominion and liberty of his country, by it' (*T* xv). In this case, Thucydides has likely instilled in Hobbes the belief that religious fervour has dangerous political consequences. This does not mean, however, that Hobbes thinks Thucydides advocates atheism. Hobbes claims that Thucydides, in a different passage, praises Nicias' worship of the gods. Perhaps one of the points Hobbes is trying to communicate here, as Lynch puts it, is that 'religion is commendable so long as it does not lead to political ruin'.[33]

The translation of Thucydides' *History of the Peloponnesian War* provides us with a glimpse into some of Hobbes's early political views, views that would have a lasting impact on him. In addition to the translation, two other sources provide information about his early politics.[34] In the first case, there is a letter, dated 18 November 1629, written to Hobbes by a person named Aglionby. The letter speaks of a manuscript, which was under investigation by the House of Lords, that was said to 'advance the liberty [of the subject] and defeat the prerogative [of the king]'.[35] Aglionby also speaks of a 'certain seditious physician called Dr. Turner one who disputes all rule, but obeys none'.[36] In this letter, Aglionby clearly reveals his disdain for the advocates of the Petition of Right. As Lynch points out, it is important to note that Aglionby speaks in a 'tone that suggests that he and Hobbes were in agreement'.[37] An additional piece of evidence for Hobbes's early support of Charles comes from his strong ties with ardent royalists. Hobbes graduated from Oxford in 1608, after which he was employed by William Cavendish to be a tutor to his son, who was also named William. After the death of both Williams in 1626 and 1628, respectively, Hobbes briefly sought other means of employment. He was then rehired by the Cavendish family to tutor yet another William Cavendish, the third Earl of Devonshire. The Cavendish family members were firm supporters of the royalist cause, especially the third Earl of Devonshire, who not only supported the King financially and politically, but had nominated Hobbes for election to the Short Parliament in 1640. The strong ties to the Cavendish family and Hobbes's nomination to the Short Parliament provide further evidence for his early commitment to the cause of King Charles.

By 1629, then, one can already discern some of the elements of Hobbes's mature political philosophy. It is clear that Hobbes, by the time he had published the translation of Thucydides' work, was already an advocate of a monarchical form of government. In addition, although Hobbes does not specifically adhere to political absolutism, it is safe to say he believed in the benefits of a strong, if not absolute, sovereign power. By this time, Hobbes also began to recognize that civil disorders often have ideological roots. My analysis has further suggested that Hobbes's political agenda probably directed him toward specific theoretical opinions concerning the nature and use of political power. More specifically, Hobbes's aims of supporting King Charles I, of teaching people about the dangers of democracy, and of counteracting the influence of demagogues, naturally lead to political absolutism, a preference for monarchy, and to an ideological solution to civil disorder. The analysis suggests, in other words, that Hobbes's political agenda influenced his political philosophy to a certain extent.[38] The political influence, however, extends beyond politics and into natural philosophy. To reveal this influence, I must continue further into Hobbes's political agenda.

3.3 Against the Seducers and Demagogues

Hobbes's political philosophy, as we have seen, is specifically designed to present a new kind of political doctrine, one that provides an alternative to the destructive opinions of 'seducers of various sorts'. A primary element of Hobbes's political agenda, then, is his critique of the ideas and actions of these seducers. Who exactly are these seducers and what do they do and say that is so destructive? Our investigation into historical events of the 1620s revealed some of the possible suspects. In his own historical works, namely *Behemoth* and *A Dialogue between a Philosopher and a Student of the Common Laws*, Hobbes specifically names the culprits responsible for civil disorder in England. The seducers are divided into three general types: (1) religious leaders, (2) Aristotelians, (3) common lawyers. In the following discussion of these groups, I rely upon Hobbes's historical works, which were written a long time after *Elements of Law*, *De Cive* and *Leviathan*. It will be shown, however, that Hobbes's concern with the seducers is not only revealed in these later historical works, but that it is already an important aspect of his earlier works in political philosophy. In addition, our previous historical investigation may be useful in showing that the main elements of Hobbes's political agenda remained constant from his first to last publication.

3.3.a Religious Leaders

Religion and politics are so intricately linked in the early modern period that it is virtually impossible to ignore the religious elements of the conflicts and wars that ravaged Europe in the sixteenth and seventeenth centuries. Hobbes's England is no exception. Hobbes, as we have seen, probably recognized the dangerous consequences of religious fervour early in his literary career. In his own history of the English Civil War, however, this recognition becomes explicit when Hobbes places most of the blame for political unrest on religious leaders, who sow disorder by creating situations of divided loyalty between God and king. In *Behemoth*, Hobbes lists six types of seducers, the first three of which are different kinds of religious leaders (B 6.167).[39] The first group includes Presbyterians, the second group includes Papists, and the third group includes a variety of religious leaders who advocate freedom of religion, e.g., Independents, Anabaptists, Quakers, Adamites and others.

The first group of religious seducers are Presbyterian preachers who, as Hobbes claims, refer to themselves as 'ministers of Christ' and 'God's ambassadors' (B 167). These ministers claim to 'have a right from God to govern everyone in his parish, and their assembly the whole nation' (B 167). The aim of these preachers is to satisfy their own ambitious desires for power and riches.

> The mischief proceeded wholly from the Presbyterian preachers, who, by a long practiced histrionic faculty, preached up the rebellion powerfully ... To the end that the State becoming popular, the Church might be so too, and governed by an Assembly; and by consequence, as they thought, seeing politics are subservient to religion, they might govern, and satisfy not only their own covetous humour with riches, but also their

malice with power to undo all men that admired not their wisdom. (*B* 363)

The 'histrionic faculties' by which preachers imbue their criminal ideas are not unambiguously spelled out by Hobbes. Nevertheless, he does clearly state that many preachers are effective progenitors of beliefs due to the dramatic ability to appear divine and 'god-like':

> And first, for the manner of their preaching; they so framed their countenance and gesture at their entrance into the pulpit, and their pronunciation both in their prayer and sermon, and used the Scripture phrase (whether understood by the people or not), as that no tragedian in the world could have acted the part of a right godly man better than these did. (*B* 193)

Hobbes believes preachers do not instill beliefs by using reason or argument, nor do they necessarily seek to teach people to understand. Instead, they indoctrinate their listeners with principles for action. For Hobbes, preachers are actors who bedazzle their audience by appearing to be divinely inspired. The doctrine of transubstantiation and the presumption of clerical power to remit sins, for example, are employed by preachers to convince people that the clergy are touched by divinity (*B* 182–3). One of the interlocutors in *Behemoth* says certain mysterious actions of the preachers 'would have an effect on me, to make me think them gods, and to stand in awe of them as of God himself' (*B* 183). Hobbes also claims many 'fruitless and dangerous doctrines' are adopted by people because they are 'terrified and amazed by preachers' (*B* 252). It was in such a manner that the 'Presbyterian ministers, throughout the whole war, instigated the people against the King' (*B* 362–3).

The second group of seducers include 'Papists', i.e., those who hold the 'belief that we ought to be governed by the Pope, whom they pretend to be the vicar of Christ, and, in the right of Christ to be governor of all Christian people' (*B* 167). Papists do not directly challenge sovereign rulers, according to Hobbes, but they frequently use their 'spiritual power' to restrict and undermine the 'temporal power' of the sovereign. The pope's spiritual power is the 'power to determine points of faith, and to be judges in the inner court of conscience of moral duties, and a power to punish those men, that obey not their precepts, by ecclesiastical censure, that is, by excommunication' (*B* 171). Temporal power, on the other hand, belongs to the sovereign and it 'consists in judging and punishing those actions that are done against the civil laws' (*B* 171). Regarding the temporal power, the Papists 'do not pretend to it directly, but only indirectly, that is to say, so far forth as such actions tend to the hindrance or advancement of religion and good manners' (*B* 171). The problem, of course, is that the pope may extend spiritual power to such a degree that it infringes upon and restricts the scope of temporal power. With such a thought in mind, one of the speakers in *Behemoth* asks: 'What power then is left to Kings and other civil sovereigns, which the Pope may not pretend to be his *in ordine ad spiritualia*?' (*B* 171). 'None, or very little' is the response. Hobbes elaborates upon this point by revealing a number of 'rights that the Pope pretended to in the kingdoms of other princes' (*B* 172).

> First, an exemption of all priests, friars, and monks, in criminal causes, for the cognizance of civil judges. Secondly, collation of benefices on whom he pleased, native or stranger, and exaction of tenths, first fruits, and other payments. Thirdly, appeals to Rome in all causes where the Church could pretend to be concerned. Fourthly, to be the supreme judge concerning the lawfulness of marriage, that is concerning the hereditary succession of Kings. (*B* 172–3)

In all of these cases, Hobbes believes the pope crosses the boundary between the spiritual and temporal orders.

The most damaging right claimed by popes, however, is the right of 'absolving subjects of their duties, and of their oaths of fidelity to their lawful sovereigns, when the Pope should think fit for the extirpation of heresy' (*B* 173). The Papists, just as the Presbyterians, create situations of divided loyalty by infringing on the temporal power of civil sovereignty.

> This power of absolving subjects of their obedience, as also that of being judge of manners and doctrine, is as absolute a sovereignty as is possible to be; and consequently there must be two kingdoms in one and the same nation, and no man be able to know which of the masters he must obey. (*B* 173)

Since the pope can absolve a subject's duty of obedience to a civil sovereign, circumstances may arise in which individuals have conflicting duties to both pope and civil sovereign.

The third type of religious seducers includes a variety of groups: Independents, Anabaptists, Quakers, Adamites and others. These religious groups sprouted from a 'controversy between the Papists and the Reformed Church that caused every man, to the best of his power, to examine by the Scriptures, which of them was in the right' (*B* 190). The debate between Protestantism and Catholicism, in other words, led individuals to read and interpret the Bible for themselves. The result was that 'every man became a judge of religion, and an interpreter of the Scriptures' and so 'they thought they spoke with God Almighty, and understood what he said' (*B* 190). The 'license of interpreting the Scripture', Hobbes says, 'was the cause of so many several sects, as have lain hid till the beginning of the late King's reign, and did then appear to the disturbance of the commonwealth' (*B* 191). As might be expected, the commonwealth is disturbed precisely because private interpretation of Scripture results in a situation of divided loyalty. If people 'speak with God' directly, then each person may decide for him or herself what civil laws are contrary to God's word, and thereby what laws may be justly broken.

In all three cases, Hobbes believes religious leaders create dissension in the commonwealth by creating situations of divided loyalty. In the first two cases, a person, or group of persons, pretends to a right from God to be spiritual leader of all Christians. In the third case, the interpretation of Scriptures is the responsibility of individuals, a situation that again raises the possibility of conflicting duties. For these reasons, religious leaders are partly responsible for the disorders in the commonwealth.

In *Behemoth*, Hobbes explicitly discusses the political problems that he probably recognized back in 1629, when he published his translation of Thucydides' work. The same issues were also a constant concern in the intervening years, as is evidenced by their presence in Hobbes's political philosophy. In *Leviathan*, for example, Hobbes says 'there have been Doctors, that hold there be three Soules in a man; so there be also that think there may be more Soules, (that is, more Sovereigns) than one, in a Commonwealth' (*L* 29.370). Such people set up a 'Ghostly Authority against the Civil' by 'working on men's minds, with words and distinctions, that of themselves signify nothing, but bewray (by their obscurity) that there walketh (as some think invisibly) another Kingdom, as it were a Kingdome of Fayries in the dark' (*L* 29.370). As he does in *Behemoth*, Hobbes claims in *Leviathan* that situations of divided loyalty based upon religion are religiously and civilly destructive.

> Now seeing it is manifest, that the Civil Power, and the Power of the Common-wealth is the same thing; and that Supremacy, and the Power of making Canons, and granting Facultyies, implyeth a Common-wealth; it followeth, that where one is Sovereign, another Supreme; where one can make laws, and another make Canons; there must needs be two Common-wealths of one and the same Subjects; which is a Kingdome divided in itself and cannot stand. For notwithstanding the insignificant distinction of

Temporall, and *Ghostly*, they are still two Kingdomes, and every Subject is subject to two Masters. (*L* 29.370)

In the *Elements of Law*, written in 1640, Hobbes describes the same problem in the following terms:

And the difficulty is this: we have amongst us the Word of God for the rule of our actions; now if we shall subject ourselves to men also, obliging ourselves to do such actions as shall be by them commanded; when the commands of God and men shall differ, we are to obey God rather than man: and consequently the general obedience to man is unlawful. (*El* 6.144–5)

With a clear reference to religious seducers, Hobbes states the problem is created by those Christians who want to place the interpretation of Scripture into individual hands or into an independent religious assembly:

This difficulty therefore remains amongst, and troubleth, those Christians only, to whom it is allowed to take for the sense of Scripture that which they make thereof, either by their own private interpretation, or by the interpretation of such as are not called thereunto by the sovereign of the commonwealth requiring a power in matters of religion either above the power civil, or at least not dependent upon it. (*El* 6.145)

Such passages, taken from his works on political philosophy, confirm that Hobbes consistently maintained the same concerns as those in the historical writings.

3.3.b Aristotelians

In *Behemoth*, Hobbes does not devote much space to a criticism of Aristotelian ideas. Yet the little he does present is quite instructive.

In this work, Hobbes briefly describes the way in which Aristotle's ideas are used to undermine the authority of the civil sovereign. The Aristotelian ideas that are criticized may be divided into three types: metaphysical, political and ethical. In this section, I will explain Hobbes's position and then reveal the political reasons he has for rejecting many of Aristotle's metaphysical, political and ethical ideas.

The primary problem with Aristotle's metaphysical ideas, according to Hobbes, is the manner in which they are used by priests to 'puzzle and entangle men with words, and to breed disputation' (*B* 215). Aristotle's doctrine of 'separated essences', for example, is used to explain the transubstantiation of the Eucharist. In the case of transubstantiation, priests claim that a piece of bread is infused with the separated essence of Christ and is thereby transformed into the 'body of Christ'. Such an event, according to Hobbes, gives the impression that priests possess godly powers and therefore deserve reverence:

> [T]he philosophy of Aristotle was made an ingredient in religion, as serving for a salve to a great many absurd articles, concerning the nature of Christ's body, and the estate of angels and saints in heaven; which articles they thought fit to have believed, because they bring, some of them profit, and others reverence to the clergy, even to the meanest of them. For when they shall have made the people believe that the meanest of them can make the body of Christ; who is there that will not both show them reverence, and be liberal to them or the Church. (*B* 215)

Priests use the metaphysical doctrines of Aristotle to convince people 'there is but one way to salvation, that is, extraordinary devotion and liberality to the Church, and a readiness for the Church's sake, if it be required, to fight against their natural and lawful sovereign' (*B* 217). Such devotion to the Church, in other words, creates the problematic situation of divided loyalty.

Hobbes's censure of Aristotle's metaphysics, then, does not need to be interpreted as driven solely by a scientific or theoretical concern. Instead, Hobbes clearly recognizes the politically dangerous implications of Aristotle's metaphysics. The philosophical critique of Aristotelian metaphysics is a political attack on the dangerous ideas that inspire religious seducers.[40]

With regard to Aristotle's political writings, Hobbes says extremely little in *Behemoth*. What he does say is that people began to study Aristotle's politics after having been acquainted with the study of Greek and Latin. Some people, Hobbes claims, had 'grown wary of the insolence of the priests' and so turned to the study of the Scriptures in the classical languages to check on the truth of what they were being taught. From the study of these languages, people became exposed to the 'democratic' ideas of Aristotle:

[People] began to search the sense of Scriptures as they are in the learned languages; and consequently studying Greek and Latin, became acquainted with the democratical ideas of Aristotle and Cicero, and from the love of their eloquence fell in love with their politics, and that more and more, until it grew into the rebellion we now talk of. (*B* 218)

Unfortunately, in this passage, Hobbes does not explain how Aristotle's political ideas are democratic, since it is difficult to interpret Aristotle as a defender of democracy. Nevertheless, Hobbes's criticism of Aristotle's politics is based upon a criticism of democracy.[41]

The brief discussion of Aristotle in *Behemoth* concludes with a critique of Aristotelian ethics. According to Hobbes, followers of Aristotle 'estimate virtue, partly by a mediocrity of the passions of men, and partly by that they are praised' (*B* 218). In the first case, Hobbes is referring to Aristotle's view of virtue as a mean state between two extremes. To determine what is virtuous in a particular situation, one must find the appropriate mean state. In the second case, Hobbes seems to think that Aristotelian virtue is also determined by subjective appraisals: 'For [according to Aristotle] several men praise several customs, and that which is virtue with one, is blamed by others; and contrarily, what one calls vice, another calls virtue, as their present affections lead them' (*B* 220). One of the consequences of Aristotle's view, in Hobbes's eyes, is that it encourages individuals to decide for themselves what is virtuous and what is vicious. The political problem with this view, as might be expected, is that it leads to a questioning of the validity of the civil law, and it thereby could foment resistance and rebellion.

This analysis has shown that Hobbes is critical of Aristotle's metaphysics because of its (mis)use by religious seducers, of Aristotle's politics because of its democratic implications, and of Aristotle's ethics because it implies that individuals subjectively determine ethical norms. All three of these points are found not only in *Behemoth*, but also in Hobbes's works in political philosophy. Throughout *Leviathan*, for example, Hobbes chastises the 'Schooles', which are 'grounded upon certain texts of Aristotle', for their use of 'insignificant speech' (*L* 2.87). In the process of condemning Aristotle's political philosophy in the *Elements of Law*, Hobbes sheds light on the mystery of how the classical philosopher promotes democratic ideas. Aristotle 'putteth so much difference between the powers of men by nature, that he doubteth not to set down, as the ground of his politics, that some men are by nature worthy to govern, and others by nature ought to serve' (*El* 7.88). Although the postulate of natural inequality seems to support an aristocratic form of government, Hobbes believes such a postulate has 'weakened the whole frame of his [Aristotle's] politics' since it has 'given men colour and pretences, whereby to disturb and hinder the peace of another' (*El* 7.88). Many individuals who believe they are naturally superior, Hobbes says, use Aristotle's words as a rationale to usurp political power (*El* 7.88). In *Leviathan*, Hobbes castigates 'Aristotle and other Heathen Philosophers' because they 'define Good, and Evill, by the Appetite of men' which is a 'Doctrine, not only Vain, but also Pernicious to the Publique State' (*L* 46.697).

3.3.c Common Law Lawyers

Hobbes discusses the wayward and factious ideas of common law lawyers in *A Dialogue between a Philosopher and a Student of the Common Laws of England*. In this work, Hobbes places some of the blame for civil strife on Sir Edward Coke, and other common law lawyers, who proclaim the law circumscribes the powers of the king. As we have seen, one of the causes of rising political tensions in the 1620s was Charles' ardent hold of his prerogative power, which could be exercised outside of legal constraints. With regard to some of Coke's views, Hobbes is in agreement. 'I agree with Sir Edward Coke', Hobbes remarks, 'when he says that reason is the soul of the law; and . . . that nothing is law that is against reason; and that reason is the life of the law, nay the common law itself is nothing else but reason' (*D* 4). Hobbes, however, disagrees with Coke's notion that the common law is an 'artificial perfection of reason, gotten by long study, observation and experience, and not every man's natural reason' (*D* 14). This artificial reason, for Coke, specifically belongs to certain learned people, e.g., judges and lawyers, who have applied themselves to the study of law. The student in Hobbes's dialogue gives the following definition of common law, which he attributes to Sir Edward Coke:

[I]f all the reason that is dispersed into so many heads, were limited into one, yet could he [i.e., the King] not make such a law as a law of England is, because by many successions of ages it hath been fined and refined by an infinite number of grave and learned men. And this it is, he [i.e., Coke] calls common law. (*D* 14)

The common law, in other words, is refined and determined over the course of time by the application of an 'artificial reason' possessed only by wise lawyers and judges.

To illustrate the dangerous political consequences of Coke's view of common law, Hobbes refers to a specific example from English politics. As was mentioned in Section 3.1, Hobbes believes the immediate cause for Charles' inability to maintain the sovereign power was his lack of funds. As it turns out, Charles I requested money from Parliament, a request denied on the basis, in part, of certain statutes claiming that kings shall not levy taxes or enact other means of funding without the 'common consent of the realm' and without the 'good will and assent of the archbishops, bishops, earls, barons, knights, burgesses, and other freemen of the land' (D 13). The interpretation of these statutes according to the 'reason' of the lawyers in Parliament, Hobbes says, is partly to blame for the failure of the King to receive needed funding.

> And when there is a Parliament, if the speaking and leading men should have a design to put down monarchy, as they had in the Parliament which began to sit the third of November, 1640, shall the King, who is to answer to God Almighty for the safety of the people, and to that end is intrusted with the power to levy and dispose of the soldiery, be disabled to perform his office, by virtue of these acts of Parliament which you have cited? If this be reason, it is reason also that the people be abandoned, or left at liberty to kill one another, even to the last man. (D 14)

As with the religious seducers, common law lawyers often create situations of divided loyalty. In their interpretation of the law, lawyers such as Coke sometimes believe the 'law' is contrary to the dictates of the king. In such situations, does one's duty to the law (as interpreted by the 'wise men' of Parliament) override one's duty to the king? Such questions, Hobbes believes, inevitably lead to division in the commonwealth and this, in turn, leads to factions and civil discord.

Hobbes, it should be noted, launches the same criticisms against common law lawyers in his treatises on political philosophy. One of the opinions 'repugnant to the nature of a Common-wealth', Hobbes says in *Leviathan*, is 'that he that hath the Sovereign Power, is subject to the Civill Laws' (*L* 29.367). In this work, Hobbes claims that 'to be subject to the Lawes, is to be subject to the Representative, that is, to himselfe; which is not subjection, but freedome from the Lawes' (*L* 29.367). One of the opinions that 'disposeth men to rebellion', Hobbes claims in *Elements of Law*, is 'that the sovereign is in such a sort obliged to his own laws' (*El* 8.172). In *De Cive*, the 'fourth opinion adversary to civil society, is their's who hold, *that they who bear rule are subject also to the civil laws*' (*Ci* 12.247). Hobbes's political philosophy also reveals his contempt for the common law lawyers' notion of reason. 'And when men think themselves wiser than all the others, clamor and demand right Reason for judge', Hobbes says, they 'seek no more, but that things should be determined by no other man's reason but their own' (*L* 5.111). Such a view is 'as intolerable in the society of men, as it is in play after trump is turned, to use for trump one every occasion, that suite whereof they have the most in their hand' (*L* 5.111–2).

3.4 Conclusion

The investigation into Hobbes's political agenda has provided support for the political interpretation of his philosophy. As I discussed in the first chapter, advocates of the political interpretation believe a proper grasp of Hobbes's political argument requires knowledge of his political agenda. According the philosophical interpretation, by contrast, Hobbes's political philosophy attempts to scientifically demonstrate truths about politics and the commonwealth, thus the specific historical goals of his agenda are quite irrelevant. While philosophical interpreters might admit that Hobbes was encouraged to present a solution for the disorders of his time, they believe his works on political philosophy should be interpreted as philosophical arguments without consideration of the particular historical background. My inquiry shows that Hobbes, from the very start of his literary career, was very much concerned with addressing specific political problems of his time. The primary intention of the investigation into Hobbes's political agenda, however, was not meant simply to buttress the political interpretation. Instead, it was intended to complete the account of Hobbes's main political ideas. The summary of Hobbes's political philosophy, presented in the second chapter, and the discussion of his political agenda in this chapter, collectively provide an adequate account of his 'political ideas'. Since my aim is to reveal the manner in which these ideas influence his natural philosophy, an account of his political ideas was requisite. In the process, I also wanted to show that Hobbes maintained a fairly consistent political agenda throughout his life. Having presented accounts of both Hobbes's natural philosophy and his political ideas, the thesis of a political influence in his natural philosophy will be defended in the remaining chapters.

Notes

1. According to S. A. Lloyd, adherents of the coercive solution include David Gauthier, J. W. N. Watkins, C. B. Macpherson, Thomas Nagel, John Plamenatz and Quentin Skinner. See Lloyd, S. A. (1992), *Ideals as Interests in Hobbes's Leviathan: The Power of Mind over Matter*. Cambridge: Cambridge University Press, pp. 6–47.
2. Ibid., p. 26.
3. Kavka, G. (1986), *Hobbesian Moral and Political Theory*. Princeton, NJ: Princeton University Press, p. 310. Quoted from Lloyd, *Ideals as Interests*, p. 26.
4. Ibid., p. 36.
5. Ibid., p. 1.
6. Kraynack, R. P. (1990), *History and Modernity in the Thought of Thomas Hobbes*. Ithaca, NY: Cornell University Press, p. 37.
7. Ibid.

8. Ibid.

9. Ibid.

10. It is interesting to note that Hobbes's solution is somewhat paradoxical. As Kraynack says: 'The paradox of Hobbes's enterprise, then, is that he introduces his own "doctrine" in order to bring an end to doctrinal politics.' See ibid., p. 63.

11. See Martinich, A. P. (1999), *Hobbes: A Biography*. Cambridge: Cambridge University Press, Chapters 2–3.

12. Reik, M. (1977), *The Golden Lands of Thomas Hobbes*. Detroit, MI: Wayne State University Press, p. 25.

13. See Martinich, *Hobbes: A Biography*, p. 77.

14. See ibid.

15. Russell, C. (1979), *Parliaments and English Politics 1621–1629*. Oxford: Clarendon Press, p. 334.

16. Ibid., p. 335.

17. Ibid.

18. Cited in ibid., p. 348.

19. Cited in ibid., p. 362.

20. Ibid., p. 336.

21. Russell also discusses the notion of martial law and how this reveals a feeling of encroachment upon the people's liberties. See ibid., p. 336.

22. Hughes, A. (1991), *The Causes of the English Civil War*. New York: St Martin's Press, p. 90.

23. Quoted in ibid., p. 91.

24. See ibid.

25. Quoted in Russell, *Parliaments and English Politics*, p. 379.

26. Hughes, *Causes of the English Civil War*, p. 93.

27. Quoted in ibid., p. 106.

28. Russell, *Parliaments and English Politics*, p. 379–80.

29. Ibid., p. 354.

30. See ibid., p. 389.

31. Reik, *Golden Lands*, pp. 36–7.

32. Martinich, *Hobbes: A Biography*, p. 78.

33. Lynch, 'Politics in Hobbes's Mechanics', p. 302.

34. For a fuller discussion of the next two points see ibid., pp. 303–4.

35. Quoted in ibid., p. 303.

36. Ibid.

37. Ibid.

38. For a book-length discussion of the influence of Hobbes's agenda on his

political philosophy, see Steinberg, J. (1988), *The Obsession of Thomas Hobbes: The English Civil War in Hobbes's Political Philosophy*. New York: Peter Lang.

39. The remaining three groups are, respectively, defenders of democratic ideas, tradesmen who believed overthrowing the monarchy would produce prosperity, and poor individuals who wanted war for private gain. See *B* 168. In my tripartite division of Hobbes's opponents, I do not consider the tradesmen or poor individuals because these two groups play a minor role. The Aristotelians I discuss may be considered a subclass of the religious seducers and, at the same time, include defenders of democratic ideals. The common law lawyers I discuss fall under the defenders of democratic ideas.

40. See also Chapter XII of *De Cive* for further confirmation.

41. For a fuller account of Hobbes's criticisms of Aristotle's specifically political views see Laird, J. (1943), 'Hobbes on Aristotle's *Politics*', *Proceedings of the Aristotelian Society*, 43, 1–20; Johnson, C. (1985), 'The Hobbesian Conception of Sovereignty and Aristotle's Politics', *Journal of the History of Ideas*, 46, 327–47.

4

The Politics of the Philosophy of Mind

4.0 Introduction

According to the traditional interpretation of influence, the early chapters of *Leviathan* present topics that are either 'far removed' from political philosophy or, insofar as these topics are related to politics, they are merely 'preliminary' to the main argument.[1] The first five chapters of Hobbes's *magnum opus* provide an abridged version of his natural philosophy. Chapters 1–3, entitled 'Of Sense', 'Of Imagination' and 'Of the Consequence or Trayne of Imaginations', respectively, present what might be called Hobbes's 'philosophy of mind'. This account, as we shall see, provides a mechanistic and materialist view of mental phenomena. Chapter 4, entitled 'Of Speech', proffers Hobbes's theory of language, wherein one finds his commitment to nominalism and to a conventional theory of truth. The fifth chapter, 'Of Reason and Science', gives a brief recapitulation of the main aspects of his scientific methodology. These five chapters on natural philosophy are followed, in the sixth chapter, by an explication of the causes of voluntary motions. One finds the transition between natural philosophy and moral philosophy in the sixth chapter of *Leviathan*. It is in this chapter that Hobbes begins to treat of human motions in a communal setting.

Hobbes scholars traditionally interpret the first five chapters in light of their strictly philosophical nature or in terms of their preparatory role in the political argument. To be sure, not all Hobbes scholars adhere to the traditional interpretation of influence. A few scholars have de-emphasized the scientific status of these chapters by focusing on their literary and rhetorical elements.[2] Such interpretations contribute to a richer and more complete comprehension of Hobbes's philosophy by considering elements nominally ignored by advocates of the traditional interpretation. Nevertheless, the traditional interpretation of influence still holds sway in Hobbes scholarship.

By supplementing, and sometimes correcting, the traditional interpretation, we may gain a better appreciation of the depth of Hobbes's thought. The traditional interpretation certainly provides valuable insight into the influence of natural philosophy on his political philosophy. Hobbes's discovery of geometry in 1630, and his subsequent investigations into natural philosophy in the 1630s, had an obvious influence on his political thinking. His political philosophy employs the analytic–synthetic methodology of geometry, it relies upon a mechanistic and materialist account of nature, and it attempts to lay down foundational and indisputable principles in an attempt to scientifically demonstrate political conclusions. In all of these ways, the traditional interpretation is basically correct. It fails to recognize, however, the implications of the historical priority of the political ideas. Hobbes's fundamental political ideas were in place before his discovery of geometry and natural philosophy. Prior to 1630, Hobbes was already a supporter of King Charles, an advocate of monarchy, a critic of demagogues and seducers, and he was already aware of the dangers of religious fervour. Contrary to the traditional interpretation, the early chapters of *Leviathan* are important not only for the reasons stated, but also because they are filled with political relevance. In the following chapters, I argue against the view that *Leviathan* begins with topics 'far removed' from political philosophy and against the position that Hobbes's natural philosophy is simply 'preliminary' to the political argument. Hobbes's views about the nature of reality, sensation, thought, language, truth and reason are not simply used to ground a political argument, but they are themselves inherently political. In addition, I further the argument by claiming that Hobbes's political ideas influence his natural philosophy.

When I claim that Hobbes's political ideas influence his natural philosophy, I will mean one of three things, taken separately or acting in combination. First, in the words of William Lynch, I mean that Hobbes's political ideas *enable* him 'to develop a fruitful approach against the background of available approaches'.[3] Hobbes's political ideas, in other words, influence him by encouraging him not only to dismiss certain options, but also to enter new intellectual territories. According to Lynch, for example, Hobbes's concern with counteracting dangerous philosophical language encourages him to develop a fruitful philosophy of language. Second, to say political ideas influence Hobbes's natural philosophy also means that such ideas make specific theories in natural philosophy attractive to him. Hobbes's recognition of the political implications of immaterialism, as we shall see, would make a materialist ontology an attractive alternative. Third, a political influence may be discerned in Hobbes's choice of topics in his natural philosophy. Hobbes's political ideas, then, may be said to influence his natural philosophy by prompting him to seek new views, by encouraging him to accept specific views that theoretically support his political ideas, and/or by pointing out relevant topics to discuss.

While Lynch exposes the influence of 'Hobbes's political agenda on his approach to mechanical questions', I will reveal the political influence at work in other areas of Hobbes's natural philosophy.[4] In his article on this topic, Lynch claims that at least two aspects of Hobbes's natural philosophy are influenced by a political agenda: the materialist ontology and the methodological emphasis on the appropriate use of language. The influence, however, extends beyond these and into his philosophy of mind. The political influence also cuts deeply into Hobbes's philosophy of language; it reveals itself not only in Hobbes's careful attention to language, but also in specific philosophical views about language. Since Lynch provides the starting point for our investigation, a discussion of his position is called for. In Section 4.1, I present Lynch's interpretation of the political influence and I contrast it with the traditional interpretation of influence. I summarize, in Section 4.2, Hobbes's philosophy of mind. In Section 4.3, I describe the political influence operating in Hobbes's philosophy of mind. Concluding comments are then made in Section 4.4.

4.1 The Politics of Hobbes's Mechanistic Materialism

In his article on the enabling power of politics in Hobbes, Lynch culls most of his evidence from Hobbes's philosophical reproof of Descartes.[5] In 1637, Hobbes received a copy of Descartes' *Discourse on Method* from an associate. After a few years, Hobbes recorded his opinion on the French philosopher's discourse in a manuscript that was sent to Marin Mersenne. Shortly thereafter, Mersenne provided Hobbes with an original print of Descartes' *Meditations on First Philosophy*. Hobbes's objections to this work were published in 1641, along with Descartes' replies.[6] In his interpretation of the objections, Lynch presents evidence for an operative political influence in Hobbes's natural philosophy.

Hobbes's multi-faceted assault of Descartes, as Lynch claims, opens with a jab at the *cogito* argument. Descartes initiates his *Meditations* by doubting all beliefs and opinions that are not clearly and distinctly perceived. As is well known, Descartes is unable to doubt his own existence, for from the fact that one is thinking, it may be inferred that one exists. Hobbes has no problem with this foundational inference. From 'the fact that I am a thinking thing it follows that I exist', Hobbes agrees, 'since that which thinks is not nothing'.[7] Difficulties arise for Hobbes, however, when Descartes infers from his foundational truth that the essence of the existing self is an immaterial mind. Hobbes proclaims that such an inference is invalid:

But when the author adds, 'that is, I am a mind, or intelligence, or intellect, or reason,' a doubt arises. It does not seem to be a valid argument to say 'I am thinking, therefore I am thought' or 'I am using my intellect, hence I am an intellect.' I might just as well say 'I am walking therefore I am a walk'.[8]

Hobbes then attempts to prove, *contra* Descartes, that the mind depends upon the existence of a material subject:

It is quite certain that the knowledge of the proposition 'I exist' depends on the proposition 'I am thinking' as the author himself has explained to us. But how do we know the proposition 'I am thinking'? It can only be from our inability to conceive an act without a subject. We cannot conceive of jumping without a jumper, of knowing without a knower, or of thinking without a thinker. It seems to follow from this that a thinking thing is somehow corporeal.[9]

According to Lynch, Hobbes intends to 'reduce a non-material thinking self to an absurdity, showing that even Descartes must finally appeal to corporeal talk to explain the thinking self'.[10] A materialist ontology, then, grounds the philosophical rebuke of Descartes' ontological dualism.

Hobbes's materialism is also central to his rejection of Descartes' proof for the existence of God. In the *Meditations*, Descartes tries to prove that God exists from the premise that the idea of God is innate, a premise that Hobbes denies on the basis of his materialist ontology. Hobbes's philosophy of sensation, as we have seen, includes the belief that all phantasms or conceptions arise from the motions of material bodies contacting sense organs. Since God is not a material body that immediately causes motions in our sense organs, we cannot have a conception of God. According to Hobbes, 'we have no idea or image corresponding to the sacred image of God. And this is why we are forbidden to worship God in the form of an image; for otherwise we might think that we were conceiving of him who is incapable of being perceived.'[11] Hobbes's materialist theory of sensation, then, contains an implicit rebuttal of Descartes' proof for the existence of God.

In his article, Lynch reveals the political relevance of Hobbes's materialist critique of Descartes' philosophy. Political implications emerge, according to Lynch, when one considers that Descartes' philosophy may be used to support theologically subversive positions. As mentioned in the previous chapter, Hobbes reproves religious seducers for exploiting Aristotle's philosophy to proliferate politically destructive opinions. To recall, Hobbes claims the 'philosophy of Aristotle was made an ingredient in religion, as serving for a salve to a great many absurd articles, concerning the nature of Christ's body, and the estate of angels and saints in heaven' (*EW* 6.215). Ultimately, one of the political problems with Descartes' philosophy is that religious demagogues employ it to justify their seditious beliefs about the nature of God. Descartes' notion of an innate idea of God provides theoretical support for religious seducers because it strongly suggests that God's nature and, perhaps, even God's intentions, are comprehensible. Hobbes's critique, in the words of Lynch, has the 'political aim of cutting off any positive appeals to a worked out description of spirits or of God which could be employed to undermine political authority'.[12] A second problem is that Descartes' dualism encourages the use of absurd phrases, such as 'immaterial mind', that may be used to 'puzzle and entangle men with words, and to breed disputation' (*B* 215). Hobbes's materialist ontology provides a way to counteract the politically dangerous use of abstract philosophical language.

While Lynch reveals the *political relevance* of Hobbes's materialist ontology, one might ask whether such relevance indicates the presence of a *political influence*. Traditionally, Hobbes scholars discuss the debate between Hobbes and Descartes primarily in scientific or philosophical terms.[13] Any political relevance would simply be an 'implication' that flows out of natural philosophy. Lynch's interpretation, on the other hand, suggests that Hobbes's political agenda, which preceded his inquiries in natural philosophy, provided a good reason for him to accept a materialist view of reality:

> Given his recent immersion into natural philosophical disputes, we might wonder why Hobbes felt compelled to latch onto these [mechanistic and materialist] principles. Having demonstrated a prior concern with political stability and theological threats to it, it seems quite possible that Hobbes latched onto bodies in motion as an explanatory principle which might enable him to deal with spirits in material terms, thereby cutting off appeals to 'incorporeal substances.'[14]

'It seems likely, given Hobbes's political agenda', Lynch claims, that Hobbes 'was driven to embrace a thorough-going materialism coupled with a careful attention to appropriate philosophical language'.[15] For Lynch, this is an example of Hobbes's political agenda influencing or enabling his natural philosophy.

Lynch also finds political relevance in Hobbes's disapproval of Descartes' 'light of nature', a faculty that supposedly discovers certain and indubitable truths. In the following passage, Descartes describes how the light of nature compels one to judge something as true.

> I could not but judge that something which I understood so clearly was true; but this was not because I was compelled so to judge by an external force, but because a great light in the intellect was followed by a great inclination in the will, and thus the spontaneity and freedom of my belief was all the greater in proportion to my lack of indifference.[16]

In response to Descartes, Hobbes contends that 'light of nature' is not the name of a genuine faculty; it is simply a metaphorical expression. As I discussed in Chapter 2, Hobbes defines reasoning in terms of the two operations of addition and subtraction. Other than these two functions, reason has no other activity to perform. Furthermore, Hobbes argues that the psychological fact that one feels compelled to accept a specific belief does not confirm the truth of that belief.

> The phrase 'a great light in the intellect' is metaphorical, and so has no force in the argument. Moreover, anyone who is free from doubt claims he has such a 'great light' and has no less strong a propensity of the will to affirm what he has no doubt about than someone who possesses real knowledge. Hence this 'light' can explain why someone obstinately defends or holds on to a given opinion, but it cannot explain his knowledge of its truth.[17]

According to Hobbes, then, the 'light of nature', even if it did exist, could only explain why a person adheres to a certain opinion. It does not allow one to determine whether the opinion is true or false.

The 'light of nature', according to Lynch, is the 'most dangerous part of Descartes' philosophy' because it 'allows for absurd and injurious challenges to peace based upon individual certainty which has nothing to do with reason'.[18] In Chapter 29 of *Leviathan*, Hobbes enumerates the 'Diseases of a Commonwealth that proceed from the poyson of seditious doctrines' (*L* 29.365). One of these doctrines is that 'every man is Judge of Good and Evil actions' (*L* 29.365). 'From this false doctrine,' Hobbes says, 'men are disposed to debate with themselves, and dispute the commands of the commonwealth; and afterwards to obey, or disobey them, as in their private judgments they see fit' (*L* 29.365). Descartes' notion of the light of nature, as Aristotle's doctrine of the mean, provides theoretical support for seducers by justifying the appeal to an inner source of certainty.

Lynch, I believe, successfully shows that Hobbes has political reasons that could have motivated him toward a materialist ontology and proper language usage. Materialism provides theoretical support for Hobbes's aspersions on the illicit use of speech for politically subversive ends. In addition, his critique of the Cartesian 'light of nature' undermines the politically dangerous notion of a private conscience. For these reasons, Lynch surmises that Hobbes 'was driven' to accept such metaphysical views on account of his political agenda. What reasons do we have for accepting Lynch's interpretation in this case? To answer this question, an elaboration upon the differences between the traditional interpretation and Lynch's view would be helpful. I will appeal to C. B. Macpherson's description of Hobbes's discovery of geometry and the subsequent application of its method to political matters as an excellent illustration of the traditional interpretation.

In his commentary on *Leviathan*, Macpherson notes that in 1629 Hobbes was a 'forty-one-year-old classical scholar in search of a new understanding of man and government.'[19] On the 'eve of his second and eye-opening trip to the Continent, and still eleven years before he produced his first work on politics', Macpherson continues, Hobbes was 'familiar with the Baconian world of ideas but apparently still searching for some more solid basis than any that Bacon's experimental and inductive thinking seemed to offer'.[20] At this point, Hobbes was 'conscious of the political instability of English society and the English state' and possessed an 'ingrained desire for security'.[21] It was during Hobbes's second trip to the continent that 'geometry hit him,' as Macpherson says.[22] Of course, Hobbes's 'search for a method and a basic hypothesis still had some way to go'.[23] Nevertheless, Hobbes was excited by geometry because of its epistemological consequences. The 'method of reasoning', Macpherson explains, 'captivated Hobbes' because the 'method enabled one to demonstrate the truth of some complex and at first sight quite unlikely propositions which everyone would agree were obviously true'.[24] Hobbes was fascinated, in other words, because 'it was a way to get *certain* results'.[25]

After being entranced by the method of geometry, Macpherson continues, Hobbes eventually became aware of the possibility of its application to political matters. Yet he recognized that geometry alone is not sufficient to ground a political philosophy. What is required to accomplish such a task is a fundamental ontological principle.

> How soon Hobbes made the connection in his own mind between the certainty of the method of geometry and the uncertainty of current moral and political theory we cannot be sure. He had clearly made it by 1640, when he had composed the *Elements of Law, Natural and Politic*. But something more than his discovery of Euclid was needed before he could apply anything like a geometrical deductive method to politics. What was needed was a basic hypothesis about the nature of things.[26]

Hobbes found the needed hypothesis, according to Macpherson, in 'those intervening years, probably in the course of his third continental trip when he became a member of the flourishing circle of scientists'.[27] The hypothesis, Macpherson continues, 'was that everything, including human sensation, is caused by motion, or more accurately, by differences in motion'.[28] The materialist and mechanistic view of nature leads Hobbes to his 'science of politics': 'Hobbes had become so obsessed by the idea of motion, and fortunately so, for it led him to his great innovation in the science of politics.'[29]

Macpherson correctly says that Hobbes's 'obsession' with the science of motion led to a 'great innovation'. Yet this is only part of the story. Three specific examples reveal that Macpherson's reading emphasizes the scientific nature of Hobbes's political philosophy. First, Macpherson claims it was the 'method of reason' which 'captivated Hobbes' because of its ability to provide 'certain results'. The implication here is that Hobbes was excited about geometry because of its scientific nature. Second, in order to apply the method of geometry to politics, Macpherson claims Hobbes needed a 'scientific hypothesis', which he just happened to find. Apparently,

Hobbes had been searching for such a hypothesis out of a desire, present in him in 1629, to find a 'new understanding of man and government'. This implies that Hobbes's primary motivation was to 'understand', rather than to offer a solution. Third, Macpherson claims it was the 'scientific obsession' with motion that 'led' to Hobbes's 'great innovation in the science of politics'. In this case, Macpherson focuses on the influence of Hobbes's scientific obsession on his political philosophy.

Lynch's view does not oppose the traditional interpretation so much as it supplements it. Certainly, Hobbes's political thinking was greatly affected by his interest in natural philosophy, as we have seen in Chapter 2. Nevertheless, as Lynch informs us, there is evidence for an opposing influence. In the following sections and chapters, I expand on the ways in which Hobbes's political ideas influence his natural philosophy. I have organized my own treatment of Hobbes's natural philosophy according to the order of their presentation in *Leviathan*. In the following sections of this chapter, I deal with the politics of Hobbes's philosophy of mind. Although I rely upon *Leviathan* for the organizational structure of my interpretation, I will cull information from other sources in cases where so doing will shed more light on Hobbes's views.

4.2 Hobbes's Philosophy of Mind

The first three chapters of *Leviathan* present the main elements of Hobbes's philosophy of mind. These chapters discuss the nature and causes of mental phenomena. In the first chapter, which is entitled 'Of Sense', Hobbes claims that the origin of all thoughts is sensation: 'For there is no conception in man's mind which hath not at first totally, or by parts, been begotten upon by the organs of Sense' (*L* 1.85). Hobbes presents his readers with a strictly materialist account of sensation, according to which sensation is not only caused by physical motions, but is itself nothing but motions. The 'cause of Sense' *is* the 'Externall Body, or Object, which presseth the organ proper to each Sense' (*L* 1.85). The pressure that is applied to the sense organs by the object is *either* immediate or mediate. In taste and touch, for example, the external object operates directly upon sense organs. When an individual sees or hears an object, by contrast, the object acts through a medium. In all cases of sensation, the applied physical pressure commences a series of internal motions that 'by the mediation of Nerves, and other strings, and membranes of the body' is carried to the 'Brain, and Heart' wherein a 'resistance, or counter-pressure' is produced (*L* 1.85). Hobbes identifies the counter-pressure and internal motions with the various sense impressions of colours, sounds, textures and the like. Sensible qualities of external objects, Hobbes says, are nothing 'but so many several motions on the matter, by which it presseth our organs diversely. Neither in us that are pressed, are they anything else other, but divers motions' (*L* 1.86).

A representational theory of perception accompanies the materialist account of sensation. Every thought, Hobbes says, is a '*Representation* or *Appearance*, of some quality, or other Accident of a body without us; which is commonly called an Object' (*L* 1.85). Although Hobbes does not explicitly distinguish between primary and secondary qualities (in Locke's sense), it seems clear from the context that representations and ideas are secondary qualities. The sense qualities that we perceive, Hobbes says, are not in the objects themselves: 'For if those Colours, and Sounds, were in the Bodies, or Objects that cause them, they could not bee severed from them' (*L* 1.86). 'The object is one thing,' Hobbes says, 'the image or fancy is another' (*L* 1.86). Hobbes implies, however, that the material or extensional qualities of objects, insofar as they impinge upon our sense organs, must be in the objects themselves. Here, Hobbes anticipates Locke's distinction between primary and secondary qualities.

The account of perception given thus far might seem to be a sense data theory of perception, according to which the immediate objects of perception are our own ideas. A problem with this view is that it erects a 'veil of perception' between the perceiver and the external object. If the immediate objects of perception are our own ideas, in other words, then the existence of the external world is called into question. In *De Corpore*, however, Hobbes implies that the object of sense is not our own ideas, but the body itself. The 'object of sight, properly called,' Hobbes says, 'is neither light nor colour, but the body itself which is lucid, or enlightened, or coloured. For light and colour, being phantasms of the sentient, cannot be accidents of the object' (*Co* 25.404). Shortly thereafter Hobbes says that the 'object is the thing received; and it is more accurately said, that we see the sun, than that we see the light' (*Co* 25.391). Hobbes is asserting that we do have access to the bodies themselves, although we perceive them as having certain qualities that they do not actually possess. If I perceive an apple, for example, I perceive the apple itself, but I see it *as* red, taste it *as* sweet, or feel it *as* hard. The apple itself, however, is not red, sweet or hard.

Despite the ambiguity surrounding Hobbes's account of perception, the main philosophical goals of this account come out quite clearly. As Deborah Hansen Soles notes:

What he [Hobbes] wants to do is provide his audience a materialist understanding of that on which they have already this pretheoretical hold. As is exemplified in the above passage, he uses 'appearance' and 'image' and related expressions to perform several jobs: to insist that ideas do not have their own special kind of reality (an immaterial reality); to introduce or reinforce the view that the way things in the world seem to be to us is the result of various materialist causal operations; that ideas are not the result of any immediate (and correct) awareness of these things; and to emphasize the fact that these ideas are representations of external objects, not the objects, or the parts of objects, themselves.[30]

In Chapter 1, then, Hobbes provides a materialist and representational theory of perception according to which ideas are representations of the qualities of external objects, representations that are caused by the motions of these objects. It also includes a materialist theory of mind in which mental phenomena are identified with physical motions.[31]

The second chapter of *Leviathan* further elaborates upon mental phenomena by discussing the nature of imagination, which includes memory, experience, dreaming and understanding. Hobbes defines imagination as 'nothing but decaying sense' (*L* 2.88). According to this definition, the imagination is simply the continuation of motions that were originally caused by the pressure exerted by external objects: 'For after the object is removed, or the eye shut, we still retain an image of the thing seen, though more obscure than when we see it. And this is it, the Latines call *Imagination*' (*L* 2.88). When sense motions become 'fading, old, and past, it is called Memory' (*L* 2.89). 'Imagination and Memory', therefore, are 'but one thing, which for diverse considerations hath divers names' (*L* 2.89). As memories collect, one gains *experience*, which Hobbes defines as 'much memory, or memory of many things' (*L* 2.89). The motions of the imagination continue while individuals sleep, and these motions constitute dreaming.

> And because in sense, the Brain, and Nerves, which are the necessary Organs of sense, are so benumbed in sleep, as not easily to be moved by the action of Externall Objects, there can happen in sleep, no Imagination and therefore no Dreame, but what proceeds from the agitation of the inward parts of mans body. (*L* 2.90)

Memory, experience and dreams, then, are all mental phenomena classified under the imagination. In addition to these three, Hobbes also places 'understanding' within the realm of the imagination. 'The imagination that is raised in man,' Hobbes says, 'by words, or other voluntary signs, is that we generally called Understanding' (*L* 2.93). Understanding is common to humans and animals since it is simply the raising of certain conceptions in the mind. A dog understands a master's call, Hobbes implies, in the sense that the call gives rise to a certain conception in the dog's mind. What distinguishes human and animal understanding, according to Hobbes, is the possession of language. Humans, unlike animals, use linguistic signs to exchange thoughts.

In the third chapter of *Leviathan*, which is entitled 'Of the Consequence or Trayne of Imaginations', Hobbes discusses the succession of thoughts occurring in the human mind. 'Mental discourse' is defined as the 'succession of one Thought to another' and it is bifurcated into two categories: guided or unguided (*L* 3.94). In some cases, our thoughts wander from one topic to the next without a 'passionate thought, to govern and direct them' (*L* 3.95). The succession of thoughts in dreams is often unguided in this fashion. Guided thoughts, by contrast, are 'regulated by some desire, and designe' (*L* 3.95). The 'train of regulated thoughts', Hobbes says, is 'of two kinds; One, when an effect imagined, wee seek the causes' and the 'other is when imagining any thing whatsoever, we seek all the possible effects' (*L* 3.96). If a man loses a key, for example, 'his mind runs back from place to place, and time to time, to find where and when he had it' and hopefully find the point at which the key was lost (*L* 3.96). In this case, one seeks the cause of the lost key through a succession of images guided by a specific purpose. The movement could also be directed toward a future goal as when, for example, one imagines a number of different ways to spend one's money.

An important form of guided thought is prudence, which Hobbes defines as the 'presumption of the future, contracted from the experience of time past' (*L* 3.98). Prudence is the ability to foresee various effects of a given cause based on prior experiences of the effects of a similar cause (*L* 3.97). Of course, actual 'foresight' is not possible since there is no certainty of the future. Yet, based on the fact that like causes are often followed by like effects, the more experience one has of a given type of cause and the effects it produces, the more likely one is to anticipate the actual effects of a present cause. A prudent person, in other words, has a considerable amount of experience with a certain type of cause and its corresponding effects and is thereby better equipped to conjecture about the actual consequences of a particular cause of that general type.

> Sometimes a man desires to know the event of an action; and then he thinketh of some like action past, and the events thereof one after another; supposing like events will follow like actions. As he that foresees what will become of a criminal, reckons what he has seen follow on the like crime before; having this order of thoughts, the crime, the officer, the prison, the judge, and the gallows. Which kind of thought is called, *foresight*, and *prudence*, or *providence*; and sometimes *wisdom*; though such conjecture, through the difficulty of observing all circumstances be very fallacious. (*L* 3.97)

Such conjecture is 'very fallacious' because, as Hobbes explains in the *Elements of Law*, it is based on experience, and one cannot draw universal conclusions from experience: '[F]or though a man have always seen the day and night to follow one another hitherto; yet can he not thence conclude they shall do so, or they have done so eternally: *experience concludeth nothing universally*' (*El* 4.16). In addition to prudence, there is another type of 'presumption' based on experience. It is possible, Hobbes claims, not only to have a presumption of the future based on past experience, but one can also make a presumption about the past based on past experience:

> As Prudence is a presumption of the Future, contracted from the experience of time Past: So there is Presumption of things Past taken from other things (not future but) past also. *For* he that hath seen by what courses and degrees, a flourishing State hath first come into civil warre, and then to ruine; upon the sights of the

ruines of any other State, will guess, the like warre courses have been there also. But this conjecture, has the same incertainty almost with the conjecture of the Future; both being grounded only upon Experience. (*L* 3.98)

As is the case with prudence, this unnamed presumption of the past is conjectural because it is grounded upon experience.

4.3 The Political Relevance of Hobbes's Philosophy of Mind

The early chapters of Hobbes's *Leviathan*, as outlined above, present a mechanistic and materialistic account of mental phenomena and of human action. At first glance, as the traditional interpretation holds, the topics discussed in these chapters do seem 'far removed' from political matters. Insofar as they are related to the political argument, Hobbes's discussion of these topics is traditionally interpreted in light of his scientific methodology. In Charles Hinnant's opinion, for example, the importance of these chapters lies 'as much in his attempt to clear away the philosophical jargon of the past as in his effort to formulate a new theory of knowledge'.[32] F. S. McNeilly similarly believes the 'only significance [of the early chapters] is that these provide the framework within which his theories of language and method are expounded'.[33] According to many adherents of the traditional interpretation, the first three chapters of *Leviathan* contain a philosophical exposition on the nature of the mind, an exposition that is important solely because of its epistemological ramifications and because of its role in the philosophical argument. An analysis of the first three chapters, however, not only provides evidence for the traditional interpretation, but also reveals a political influence at work. To reveal this influence, I will begin by discussing the immediate political relevance of certain elements in Hobbes's natural philosophy. I will then suggest that such relevance, when conjoined with the historical priority of Hobbes's political ideas, provides evidence for the operation of a political influence.

As in his criticism of Descartes, Hobbes's materialist account of mental phenomena is not important simply for its philosophical value. Instead, the political importance of his philosophy of mind lies in the fact that it is used to debunk the metaphysical ideas of Aristotle. At the end of Chapter 1 in *Leviathan*, Hobbes criticizes the 'insignificant speech' inspired by Aristotle's metaphysics:

> But the Philosophy-schooles, through all the Universities of Christendome, grounded upon certain Texts of Aristotle, teach another doctrine; and say, For the cause of Vision, that the thing seen, sendeth forth on every side a *visible species* (in English), a *visible shew*, *apparition*, or *aspect* … I say not this, as disapproving the use of Universities: but because I am to speak hereafter of their office in a Commonwealth, I must let you see on all occasions by the way, what things would be amended in them; amongst which the frequency of insignificant speech is one. (*L* 2.87)

Hobbes's claim that the term 'visible species' embodies a form of insignificant speech is not simply a jab at Aristotle's philosophy, but it is a politically motivated criticism. As I mentioned in Chapter 3 of the present work, criticisms of Aristotle's metaphysics are politically motivated attacks on the religious seducers who use his doctrines to trick people into submission.[34] According to Hobbes, religious seducers use 'insignificant words', such as 'visible species', to bedazzle and captivate the imagination of the people. Thus, Hobbes's discussion of the mechanics of sensation is not far from political concerns, even apart from its role in the political argument of *Leviathan*. Hobbes confirms this point in the above passage when he claims the universities should be reformed.

One may also discern political relevance in Hobbes's materialist account of dreaming. A dream, to recall, is simply the continuation of motions originally caused by the 'pressing' of external objects on our sense organs. At first glance, it seems as though Hobbes might not be concerned, as a 'philosopher' should be, with the epistemological problems of dreaming. Hobbes simply says, 'I am well satisfied, that being awake, I know I dreame not; though when I dreame, I think my selfe awake' (*L* 2.90). Hobbes's dismissal of the philosophical importance of this question is probably a jab at Descartes, whose methodological doubt relies upon the possibility that waking experience is simply a dream. Insofar as a philosophical critique of Descartes' metaphysics is political, Hobbes's implied criticism has political implications. More importantly, however, Hobbes's account of dreams carries an explicit political function; it serves as a castigation of 'false prophets' who use dreams as evidence of divine power:

> If this superstitious fear of Spirits were taken away, and with it, Prognostiques from Dreams, false Prophecies, and many other things depending thereon, by which, crafty ambitious persons abuse the simple people, men would be much more fitted than they are for civill Obedience. (*L* 2.93)

In the midst of his 'scientific account' of human sensation, Hobbes clearly indicates his awareness of the political relevance of his mechanics of perception. This point is confirmed much later in *Leviathan*:

> To say he [God] hath spoken to him in a Dream, is to say no more than he dreamed that God spake to him; which is not of force to win beleef from any man, that knows that dreams are for the most part naturall, and may proceed from former thoughts; and such dreams as that, from self conceit, and foolish arrogance, and false opinions of mans own godlinesse, or other vertue, by which he thinks he hath merited that favor of extraordinary Revelation. (*L* 32.411)

The topic of dreams is important not simply because of its scientific or strictly philosophical value, but on account of its political relevance.

In a similar manner, Hobbes's view of 'experience' is replete with political relevance. Since experience is nothing but a collection of memories, it does not provide a solid basis for knowledge claims. No one can be certain that the future will resemble the past, and so any claims made on the basis of experience must remain conjectural. As an aspect of Hobbes's scientific methodology, this point seems unrelated to Hobbes's political concerns. Nevertheless, it is not. In Chapter 2, I pointed out that one of Hobbes's opponents is Sir Edward Coke, the common law lawyer. Coke, as we have seen, believes that the nature of justice is determined by an examination of the common law, which requires experience of previous sentences made by judges. According to Hobbes, the nature of justice is not to be discerned by an examination of previous court cases. This point is clearly expressed in the *Elements of Law*, which happens to be the 'more scientific' of Hobbes's political works:

> As in conjectural things concerning past and future, it is prudence to conclude from experience, what is likely to come to pass or have passed already; so it is an error to conclude from it, that it is so or so called. That is to say, we cannot from experience conclude that any thing is to be called just or unjust, true or false, nor any proposition universal whatsoever ... For example, to have heard a sentence given (in the like case the like sentence a thousand times) is not enough to conclude that the sentence is just. (*El* 5.16–17)

According to Hobbes, common law lawyers use previous decisions as a basis for determining what is 'just' and what is 'unjust'. Hobbes's view of experience undermines their attempts at determining the nature of justice on the basis of experience.

At this point, however, one should note an inconsistency

concerning Hobbes's view of experience. As we have seen, Hobbes declares himself to be the first philosopher to establish a *scientific* political philosophy grounded on *true* principles. In many places, Hobbes claims that the principles of his political philosophy are known by experience. For example, in *De Cive* Hobbes 'sets down for a principle by experience known to all men and denied by none, to wit, that the dispositions of men are naturally such, that except they be restrained by some coercive power, every man will distrust and dread each other' (*Ci* Preface 99). In the *Elements of Law*, Hobbes presents a principle that is the 'true and only foundation of such science' (*El* Epistle xvi). In so doing, Hobbes claims he is 'not intending to take any principle upon trust, but only to put men in mind of what they know already, or may know by their experience' (*El* 1.1). Hobbes claims his civil philosophy is 'grounded on its own principles sufficiently known by experience' (*Ci* Preface 103). The implication is that Hobbes's foundational principles of his science of politics may be known by experience. If political philosophy is a genuine science and if the principles of this science are true, and if these principles are known by experience, then Hobbes implies that experience does provide a legitimate basis for truth claims. Thus, Hobbes's notion that experience cannot establish truth is inconsistent with his view that experience provides the true principles of his political philosophy.

The inconsistency may be explained by noticing the political relevance behind both positions. Hobbes's political solution is to establish a science of politics grounded on indubitable principles. Such a science is needed, as we have seen, to put an end to doctrinal politics. Thus, Hobbes desires to establish a political philosophy to which everyone would agree. This task requires Hobbes to find indubitable principles that none can deny. Since the basic principles of human nature seem to be confirmed by experience, the turn to empirical evidence is natural. Experience, then, plays an important role in proving the truth of the foundational principles. At the same time, however, Hobbes is aware of the common law lawyers' use of experience to ground their assertions about the nature of justice. To combat this seditious idea, Hobbes is drawn to an alternative view, a view that denies that experience grounds truth. An appeal to the possible political motivation behind Hobbes's adoption of these views, then, provides us with a reasonable explanation as to why he landed himself in this inconsistency. As we shall see in the following chapters, many inconsistencies in Hobbes's natural philosophy may be explained in a similar fashion.

After the discussion of prudence and experience, Hobbes closes the third chapter with a few remarks on the inability of our imagination to comprehend God's nature. 'Whatsoever we imagine, is *Finite*,' Hobbes claims, '[t]herefore there is no Idea, or conception of anything we call *Infinite*' (*L* 3.99). Accordingly, we cannot have a conception of the 'incomprehensible God' (*L* 3.99). To claim one does have a conception of God, or any infinite things, is to employ 'absurd speeches, taken upon credit (without any signification at all,) from deceived Philosophers, and deceived, or deceiving Schoolemen' (*L* 3.99). While Hobbes is using his mechanistic view of sensation and imagination to criticize philosophical ideas, the political relevance of these passages must not be overlooked. For political reasons, Hobbes wants to show that no one has knowledge about God, thus no one can appeal to God's wishes in order to justify disobedience to the civil sovereign.

4.4 Conclusion

Hobbes's philosophy of sensation, dreaming and experience, then, are all politically relevant aspects of his natural philosophy. The question, of course, is whether the political relevance of these philosophical ideas provides evidence for a political influence. The evidence, to be sure, does not prove a unidirectional causal link between Hobbes's political ideas and his natural philosophy. Nevertheless, I believe it offers support for the existence of one or more of the three types of influence discussed at the start of this chapter. The issue may be clarified by discussing it in terms of counterfactual questions, such as: if Hobbes had not been concerned with political attacks on Aristotelians, religious seducers and common law lawyers, would he have adopted the same philosophical positions? Would Hobbes have included a scientific account of dreaming in a political treatise if he had not been aware of its political implications? Would he have so readily accepted a materialist ontology, which denies the existence of 'visible species', had it not been for his recognition of the dangerous use of metaphorical language? Would Hobbes have discussed the concept of God in a discourse on human imagination? Negative answers to these questions give credence to the thesis that Hobbes's political ideas influence his natural philosophy. I believe there are three reasons for answering these questions negatively.

First, according to the evidence presented by Lynch, it is reasonable to assume that Hobbes's recognition of the dangerous use of Aristotelian language and of Cartesian metaphysics made the new materialist ontology attractive to him. At the very least, then, Hobbes's political ideas provide a reason for him to accept and advocate a materialist ontology. Given Hobbes's own explicit recognition of the political implications of certain elements of his natural philosophy, one might reasonably infer that these implications were intuited by Hobbes, whether or not he consciously recognized it. The alternative is to say that Hobbes developed his natural philosophy first, and then he simply noticed how it could be used to combat his political opponents. This seems doubtful since Hobbes's original intention, one might say, was political. It was primarily on account of his political aims that he searched for ways to use his natural philosophy against his political opponents. Thus, Hobbes's own recognition of the political implications of his philosophy of sensation, imagination and experience suggests that such philosophical ideas were attractive to him for political reasons.

Second, because Hobbes was specifically concerned with combatting dangerous ideas, he included in his 'scientific' account of human nature specific topics that would ultimately help his political cause. Hobbes's view of dreaming, for example, plays no role in the political argument of *Leviathan*. In almost all interpretations of *Leviathan*, the political relevance of dreaming is entirely ignored.[35] Nevertheless, his decision to include an account of dreaming may be explained, even if only partially, by appealing to his political ideas.

Third, the view that Hobbes's political ideas influence his natural philosophy becomes more attractive as one recognizes that many of the ideas expressed in the first five chapters of *Leviathan* are extremely relevant to political matters. The case, in other words, becomes stronger when a pattern of influence is revealed. In the following chapters, I present more evidence for the existence of such a pattern.

Notes

1. See Sections 2.3 and 2.4.
2. See, for example, Cantalupo, C. (1991), *A Literary Leviathan: Thomas Hobbes's Masterpiece of Language*. Lewisburg, PA: Bucknell University Press; Johnston, D. (1986), *The Rhetoric of Leviathan: Thomas Hobbes and the Politics of Cultural Transformation*. Princeton: Princeton, NJ University Press.
3. Lynch, W. T. (1991), 'Politics in Hobbes's Mechanics: The Social as Enabling', *Studies in the History of the Philosophy of Science*, 22 (2), 298–9.
4. Ibid., p. 296.
5. Lynch also relies upon Hobbes's philosophical disagreements with Thomas White, author of *De Mundo*. See ibid.
6. In Descartes, R. (1984), *The Philosophical Writings of Descartes*, J. Cottingham, R. Stoothoff and D. Murdoch (trans.). Cambridge: Cambridge University Press, Vol. 2.
7. Ibid., p. 122.
8. Ibid.
9. Ibid.
10. Lynch, 'Politics in Hobbes's Mechanics', p. 310.
11. In Descartes, *Philosophical Writings of Descartes*, p. 127. Quoted in Lynch, 'Politics in Hobbes's Mechanics', p. 310.

12. Lynch, 'Politics in Hobbes's Mechanics', p. 311.

13. For more on Hobbes's criticisms of Descartes, see Sepper, D. (1988), 'Imagination, Phantasms, and the Making of Hobbesian and Cartesian Science', *Monist*, 71, 526–42.

14. Lynch, 'Politics in Hobbes's Mechanics', p. 308.

15. Ibid., p. 309.

16. In Descartes, *Philosophical Writings of Descartes*, p. 134. Quoted in Lynch, 'Politics in Hobbes's Mechanics', p. 310.

17. Ibid.

18. Lynch, 'Politics in Hobbes's Mechanics', pp. 302–11.

19. Macpherson, C. B. (1968), 'Introduction to *Leviathan*', in Hobbes, T., *Leviathan*, C. B. Macpherson (ed.). Harmondsworth: Penguin, p. 17.

20. Ibid.

21. Ibid.

22. Ibid.

23. Ibid.

24. Ibid.

25. Ibid., p. 18.

26. Ibid.

27. Ibid.

28. Ibid.

29. Ibid., p. 19.

30. Soles, D. H. (1996), *Strong Wits and Spider Webs: A Study in Hobbes's Philosophy of Language*. Aldershot: Ashgate Publishing, pp. 8–9.

31. For an overview of other interpretations see ibid., Chapters 1 and 2.

32. Hinnant, C. (1977), *Thomas Hobbes*. Boston, MA: Twayne Publishers, p. 101.

33. McNeilly, F. S. (1968), *The Anatomy of Leviathan*. London: St Martin's Press, p. 31.

34. See Section 3.3.

35. This is not to mention the fact that traditional interpretations of *Leviathan* overlook the philosophical relevance of Hobbes's view of dreaming, viz., the manner in which this view is a criticism of Descartes' philosophy.

The Politics of Language and Truth

5.0 Introduction

In the previous chapter, I suggested that Hobbes's philosophy of mind, as represented in the first three chapters of *Leviathan*, reveals the presence of a political influence. The fourth chapter of *Leviathan*, entitled 'Of Speech', contains what might be called Hobbes's 'philosophy of language'. Traditionally, Hobbes's philosophy of language is recognized for its important, but subsidiary, role in his political philosophy. Watkins, for example, claims that 'in *Leviathan* Hobbes's theory of language makes an early appearance, as one of the indispensable preliminaries to his civil philosophy'.[1] Rather than being a crucial component of the political problem, Hobbes's philosophy of language is 'preliminary'. Watkins recognizes, of course, that it still has 'important implications' for political philosophy.[2] Nevertheless, he does not explore the possibility that such implications indicate a political influence. M. M. Goldsmith similarly claims that Hobbes's theory of language is important because of its philosophical role in the discovery of knowledge. According to Goldsmith, to 'explain Hobbes's use of the analytic-synthetic method and his system of philosophy, some account must be given of how knowledge is possible, or how men can come to know the world, and of how they can come to explain it'.[3] An understanding of Hobbes's philosophy of language is a necessary component to such a task. In Goldsmith's book, the discussion of language is restricted to its role in achieving this task. Goldsmith and Watkins believe that Hobbes's philosophy of language is *preliminary* to the political problem, rather than a major aspect of it.

In recent years, however, Hobbes's philosophy of language has taken a more prominent place in treatments of his political philosophy. Deborah Hansen Soles, for example, claims that 'Hobbes is adamant that neither moral philosophy nor civil philosophy can be pursued in the absence of an account of language.'[4] 'Hobbes's understanding of how we go about securing knowledge about political phenomena', John Danford says, 'depends on his picture of language'.[5] In an article on the relationship between Hobbes's philosophy of language and politics, Frederick Whelan suggests that 'semantic disputes ... in politics may have figured as prominently in motivating Hobbes's elaborate theory of language'.[6] He also argues that 'it is in speech in general, and in the misuse of it, that Hobbes usually seeks and finds the proximate causes of civil disorder'.[7] Although Hobbes finds the 'ultimate source of conflict' in differing opinions, he also recognizes, in the words of Whelan, that 'verbal disputes are its most manifest and immediate cause'.[8] William Lynch, as well, emphasizes the centrality of political factors motivating Hobbes's close attention to language.[9] In contrast to advocates of the traditional interpretation, such scholars link the philosophy of language immediately to the political problem of civil disorder.

While some interpreters recognize and elaborate upon the political relevance of Hobbes's philosophy of language, the political influence operative within his philosophy of language has not been properly exposed. This influence, I believe, is partly responsible for a number of inconsistencies in Hobbes's philosophy of language. In this chapter, I provide an overview of Hobbes's philosophy of language and some of its inconsistencies. Section 5.1 contains an overview of Chapter 4 of *Leviathan*, which deals primarily with topics in the philosophy of language. In Section 5.2, I argue that there is an inherent inconsistency in Hobbes's view of truth. I will then suggest, in Section 5.3, that the thesis of a political influence provides a good explanation for this inconsistency. In following chapters, I will attempt to argue that this thesis provides the best explanation for this inconsistency, and many others, in Hobbes's natural philosophy.

5.1 Hobbes's Philosophy of Language: An Overview

In *Leviathan*, Hobbes praises human speech as the 'most noble and profitable invention of all others' (*L* 4.100). The two other inventions mentioned here are printing and letters. Although the invention of printing is 'ingenious', Hobbes says, it is of 'no great matter' when compared with that of letters, which is a 'profitable invention for continuing the memory of time past, and the conjunction of mankind' (*L* 4.100). Neither of these, however, comes close to the invention of speech, especially when one considers its benefits:

> But the most noble and profitable invention of all other, was that of Speech, consisting of *Names* or *Appellations*, and their Connexion; whereby men register their Thoughts; recall them when they are past; and also declare them one to another for mutual utility and conversation; without which, there had been amongst men, neither Common-wealth, nor Society, nor Contract, nor Peace, no more than amongst Lions, Bears, and Wolves. (*L* 4.100)

As mentioned in the summary of Hobbes's political philosophy, the commonwealth is created when individuals in a state of nature covenant with each other to authorize a sovereign power. Such a covenant, Hobbes believes, is not possible without the use of speech. Speech, then, is a central component of the political solution and, as I have already intimated, it is also at the heart of the political problem.

The 'first author of Speech', Hobbes says, 'was God himself, that instructed Adam how to name such creatures as he presented to his sight' (*L* 4.100). The Scriptures, however, do not reveal much information about the development of language beyond God's teaching Adam the names of some animals. Nevertheless, Hobbes believes this was enough to teach Adam how to name things himself and how to join names into propositions. All advance of human speech accomplished by Adam and his successors, however, 'was again lost at the tower of Babel, when by the hand of God, every man was stricken for his rebellion, with an oblivion of his former language' (*L* 4.101). After being deprived of language, humans were forced by necessity to reinvent it. In addition, since humans were dispersed at Babel, a variety of languages developed among the groups.

Although Hobbes does not explicitly mention the political significance of this biblical story, his claim that the people were punished for their 'rebellion' against God partly reveals its significance. The tower of Babel, which was built to reach into the heavens, called into question the gulf between God and human. The human 'rebellion' against God, in other words, was the decision to act on the prideful belief that humans could be divine and godlike themselves. What follows from such pride is the chaos of dispersion and the situation of everyone speaking a different language. The political significance of this story becomes apparent when we recognize its analogical character. The sovereign, Hobbes claims in *Leviathan*, is a 'Mortall God' to which we owe our obedience (*L* 17.227). When demagogues and seducers claim the rights that belong properly to the sovereign, that is, when these rebellious individuals claim their equality with the king, problems will necessarily follow. The various rebellious groups, we might say, speak a different language insofar as they use certain names, e.g., 'just' and 'good', in different ways. The punishment for one's rebellion against God, whether the mortal or immortal one, is a dissolution of the commonwealth into a state where people speak in different tongues.

After presenting his brief history of speech, Hobbes turns to the topic of its use. The 'general use of Speech', Hobbes says, is to 'transferre our Mental Discourse into Verbal' (*L* 4.101). There are two primary reasons for wanting to transfer the 'Trayne of our Thoughts, into a Trayne of Words' (*L* 4.101). First, such transference allows us to remember our thoughts by providing the means to recall them. Second, the expression of our thoughts in language permits humans to communicate their thoughts to others. Hobbes's explicit definition of 'name' suggests two primary functions, i.e., to serve as 'marks' and to serve as 'signs':

> A name is a word taken at pleasure to serve for a mark, which may raise in our mind a thought like to some thought we had before, and which being pronounced to others, may be to them a sign of what thought the speaker had, or had not before his mind. (*Co* 2.16)

Hobbes then claims that there are four 'special' uses of speech: (1) to register our thoughts, (2) to communicate our ideas to each other, (3) to inform each other of our wants and wishes, and (4) 'to please and delight ourselves, and others, by playing with words, for pleasure or ornament, innocently' (*L* 4.102).

These four uses of speech have correspondent 'abuses'. The first occurs 'when men register their thoughts wrong, by the inconstancy of the significations of their words; by which they register for their conceptions, that which they never conceived; and so deceive themselves' (*L* 4.102). If, for example, the name 'infinite' were applied to any of our conceptions, we would deceive ourselves since 'there is no Idea, or conception of anything we call *Infinite*' (*L* 3.99). Speech can also be abused, in the second case, when it is used metaphorically, that is, when words are used 'in other sense than that which they are ordained for' (*L* 4.102). In the third case, individuals can simply lie about their wants, wishes or desires. The fourth abuse happens when people use words 'to grieve one another' through insults, aspersions, satirical remarks and the like (*L* 4.102). The dangerous political consequences of the misuse of speech by seducers and demagogues have already been mentioned.[10]

Hobbes follows his discussion of the abuses of speech with a more detailed account of names. An important aspect of Hobbes's theory of names is his distinction between proper and common names. A proper name, Hobbes says, signifies an individual, while a common name signifies a number of individuals at once:

> [O]f names, some are *Proper*, and singular to one onely thing; as *Peter, John, This man*, and *this Tree*: and some are *Common* to many things; as *Man, Horse, Tree*; every of which though but one Name, is nevertheless the name of divers particular things; in respect of all which together, is called an *Universall*; there being nothing in the world Universall but Names; for things named, are every one of them Individuall and Singular (*L* 4.102)

This passage reveals Hobbes's commitment to the nominalist denial of universals.

After presenting his view of particular, common and universal names, Hobbes discusses the manner in which names are connected to each other. Names, Hobbes points out, have various levels of signification. The name *body*, for example, signifies more than does the name *man*. This is due to the fact that *body* is used to signify more conceptions than *man*. Hobbes would also say that *body* 'comprehends' *man* since the name *body* signifies all of the conceptions signified by *man*. Scientific knowledge, according to Hobbes, is made possible by the fact that names, which have different levels of signification, can be joined into propositions. To illustrate this point, Hobbes explains how speech allows one to attain universal knowledge of a triangle. If a 'man that hath not the use of speech', Hobbes says, 'set before his eyes a triangle and by it two right angles' then 'he may by meditation compare and find, that the three angles of that triangle, are equall to those two right angles that stand by it' (*L* 4.103). This speechless man knows that the two angles of this particular triangle are equal to two right angles, but 'if another triangle be shown to him different in shape from the former, he cannot know without a new labour, whether the three angles also be equal to two right angles' (*L* 4.103). A man with speech, however, can 'register' his discovery in the 'general terms, *Every triangle hath its three angles equal to two right angles*. And thus the consequence found in one particular comes to be registered and remembered' (*L* 4.104). Speech 'delivers us from the labour of the mind' and 'makes that which was found true *here*, and *now*, to be true in *all times* and *places*' (*L* 4.104). Equipped with this knowledge, in other words, the person with speech 'will boldly conclude Universally, that such equality of angles is in all triangles whatsover' (*L* 4.104).

Hobbes's view of truth depends upon the fact that names have different levels of signification. A true proposition, Hobbes claims, is one in which the predicate term 'comprehends' the subject term:

> When two Names are joyned into a Consequence, or Affirma-
> tion; as thus, *A man is a living creature*; or thus, *if he be a man, he is a*
> *living creature*. If the later name *Living creature*, signifieth all that the
> former name *Man* signifieth, then the affirmation, or conse-
> quence, is *true*; otherwise, *false*. (*L* 4.104–5)

Hobbes then informs us that truth and falsity are characteristics of propositions: 'For *Truth* and *Falsehood* are attributes of Speech and not of Things. And where speech is not, there is neither *Truth* nor *Falsehood*' (*L* 4.105). Hobbes's commitment to the propositional nature of truth is partly responsible for the scholarly attribution of a conventional view of truth to him.

The remainder of the chapter on speech may be summed up quite briefly. The treatment of truth is followed by praises of geometry, the only 'god-given science' (*L* 4.105). Since scientific demonstration requires true premises, one must begin with true propositions to prove one's conclusions scientifically. In geometry,

Hobbes says, 'men begin at settling the significations of their words; which settling of significations, they call *Definitions*' (*L* 4.105). Since definitions serve as the primary principles of any demonstration, errors at the start 'multiple themselves' and 'lead men into many absurdities' (*L* 4.105). The cautious warning to employ proper definitions is followed by a discussion of those things to which names may be applied. The 'diversity of names', Hobbes says, 'may be reduced to four general heads' (*L* 4.107). Names may be applied to (1) bodies, (2) accidents of bodies, (3) our conceptions, and (4) names themselves. Insignificant speech arises when names are improperly joined together, as in joining of the names 'incorporeall' and 'body'. In addition, Hobbes claims that understanding only occurs between people when the words they use are of 'constant signification' (*L* 4.109). Since understanding is 'nothing else but conception caused by speech', the use of names without a fixed signification often leads to misunderstanding and confusion (*L* 4.109). From the fact that names signify our conceptions and the fact that conceptions differ from person to person, Hobbes draws the conclusion that words not only signify the conceptions, but that they reveal the 'nature, disposition and interest of the speaker' (*L* 4.109). This is made manifest by the fact that individuals may have different names for the same thing: 'For one man calleth *Wisdome*, what another calleth *feare*; and one *cruelty*, what another *justice*; one *prodigality*, what another *magnanimity*; and one *gravity*, what another *stupidity*, &c' (*L* 4.109). As might be expected, Hobbes implies that such inconstant signification is quite 'dangerous' (*L* 4.110).

We must briefly pause and take a closer look at Hobbes's theory of names because there is an important problem that recurs in his account of truth. Names, as we have seen, serve either as signs or as marks of our conceptions. Because names are signs of mental conceptions, it seems that Hobbes's theory of names involves only a 'name–conception' relation. A name, in other words, signifies only conceptions in the mind. This could easily lead one to believe that names do not have any reference to the things themselves.[11] Such an interpretation is corroborated when Hobbes claims in *De Corpore* that since 'names ordered in speech (as is defined) are signs of our conceptions, it is manifest they are not signs of the things themselves' (*Co* 2.17). Despite first appearances, however, Hobbes seems to admit of a 'name–thing' relationship:

> For as these, a *man*, a *tree*, a *stone*, are the names of the things themselves, so the images of a man, of a tree, and of a stone, which are represented to men sleeping, have their names also, though they be not things, but only fictions and phantasms of things. (*Co* 2.17)

This passage suggests that names do not simply signify or mark conceptions in the mind, but they may also be used to refer to 'truly existing' things. It is easy to overlook the possibility of a name–thing relationship, as Watkins says, since Hobbes 'says almost nothing about the name–thing relation because he could not accommodate it within his causal psychology.'[12] An inconsistency arises, therefore, because Hobbes explicitly states that names have two functions, but in practice he implies a third function, i.e., naming. The question we are concerned with, then, is whether Hobbes is consistent in his discussion about the 'name–thing' and the 'name–conception' relationships.[13] Scholars traditionally address this problem by claiming that names have three separate functions for Hobbes. In the first two functions, marking and signifying, Hobbes is concerned with a name–conception relationship. In the third function, what scholars variously refer to as 'naming' or 'denoting', names refer to, or apply to, things. Watkins, for example, says that a 'name is a *sign* of the conception (in the mind of the speaker or writer) but a *name* of the thing itself'.[14] 'It is important to recognize', Deborah Hansen Soles claims, 'that Hobbes distinguishes *three* uses or functions of names: to mark, to signify, or to denote.'[15] It is clear from the above passages that Hobbes accepts a denotational function for names. The question, however, is whether Hobbes consistently maintains this tripartite division. A careful look at some passages reveals that he does not.

Although the following passage supports the interpretation that Hobbes admits of a 'name–thing' relationship, it does not give evidence for Watkins' view that *naming* always involves such a relationship.

> But seeing every name has some relation to that which is named, though that which we name be not always a thing that has a being in nature, yet it is lawful for doctrine's sake to apply the word *thing* to whatsover we name; as if it were all one whether that thing be truly existing, or be only feigned. (*Co* 2.18)

The passage clearly indicates that Hobbes believes we may give names to 'truly existing' things. At the same time, however, Hobbes implies that we may 'name' or 'apply a name' to a 'feigned' thing, i.e., a thing that has existence only in the mind. While Watkins is correct to say that Hobbes admits of a name–thing relationship, there is little evidence to suppose that Hobbes consistently distinguishes between three functions of names. In *De Corpore*, for example, Hobbes implies that a sign may be used to refer to a man, and not just the conception of a man:

> [F]or a *man* denotes anyone of a multitude of men, and a *philosopher*, any one of many philosophers, by reason of their similitude; also, *Socrates* is a positive name because it signifies always one and the same man. (*Co* 2.18)

In this case, both denoting and signifying seem to be used interchangeably. If this is the case, then Hobbes is not consistent in his terminological usage.

How shall we explain this inconsistency? One obvious explanation is to attribute carelessness or sloppy thinking to Hobbes. 'When he is being careful,' Soles says, 'Hobbes is very explicit in saying that names are not ever used to name or denote what they mark or signify.'[16] 'Unfortunately,' Soles continues, 'there are passages in which he is concerned with making some different point, and in those, he is not consistent with his more careful usage.'[17] A more satisfactory answer is given by Hungerland and Vick, who claim the problem arises from a bad translation of *De Corpore*. In 1655, *De Corpore* was published in Latin. An English translation, which was supervised and approved by Hobbes, was published one year later. According to Hungerland and Vick, there are numerous errors of translation that obscure Hobbes's theory of signification. One such error is contained in the passage quoted above, in which the English translation states that '*Socrates* is a positive name because it signifies always one and the same man' (*Co* 2.18). The Latin word that is translated as 'signifies' is *denotat*, not *significat*. Although the error occurred through translation, Hungerland and Vick ultimately explain it by reference to Hobbes's lack of focus: 'Hobbes's general carelessness, [is] shown, for example, in his approving of a translation full of mistakes.'[18]

In the following sections, I provide a different explanation for this inconsistency. I believe the inconsistency is part and parcel of a larger problem in Hobbes's philosophy of language, namely, the problem of the relating words to the world. As we have seen, Hobbes is inconsistent when it comes to describing this relationship, and this inconsistency also reveals itself in his theory of truth. Thus, I will save my explanation for later.

5.2 Hobbes's View of Truth

It is frequently pointed out, as we shall see, that Hobbes does not hold consistent views on truth. On the one hand, Hobbes seems to endorse a conventional view of truth when he explicitly discusses truth. In this case, truth is a matter of linguistic convention; it is a matter of how we use words and not necessarily about whether words genuinely reflect the way the world is. On the other hand, Hobbes seems to accept a correspondence view of truth implicitly when he claims his own philosophy is true. Here, Hobbes implies that his own philosophy accurately describes the world.

5.2.a The Conventional View of Truth

Most evidence supports the conclusion that Hobbes explicitly adheres to a conventional view of truth which states that truth is not a matter of correspondence with reality, but is a matter of conventional agreement. Much of this evidence is grounded in his view that truth is a characteristic of propositions. In *De Corpore*, Hobbes confirms the linguistic nature of truth that is expressed in *Leviathan*: 'the words *true*, *truth*, and *true proposition* are equivalent to one another; for truth consists in speech and not in the things spoken of' (*Co* 3.35). Similarly, in *The Elements of Law*, Hobbes says that 'truth, and a true proposition, is all one' (*El* 5.21). Hobbes's view in *Leviathan* that true propositions are propositions in which one term comprehends another is found in other works. In the *Elements of Law*, for example, Hobbes expresses this view:

> In every proposition, be it affirmative or negative, the later appellation either comprehendeth the former, as in this proposition, charity is a virtue, the name of virtue comprehendeth the name of charity (and many other virtues beside), and then this proposition is said to be True or Truth ... Or else the latter appellation comprehendeth not the former; as in this proposition, every man is just, the name *just* comprehendeth not every man; for *unjust* is the name of the far greater part of man. And then the proposition is said to be False or Falsity. (*El* 5.21)

To see the connection between the conventional view of truth and the claim that truth is a characteristic of propositions, it would be helpful to return to the topic of names.

Names, according to Hobbes, are assigned to various conceptions by an act of will. In some cases, Hobbes goes so far as to state explicitly that the assigning of names is a completely arbitrary matter. In the *Elements of Law*, for example, Hobbes claims that a 'name or appellation therefore is the voice of a man, arbitrarily imposed, for a mark to bring to his mind some conception concerning the thing on which it is imposed' (*El* 5.18). If the assignment of names is an arbitrary affair, then it would appear that truth itself must be arbitrary. In *De Corpore*, Hobbes explicitly shows the connection between the arbitrary assignment of names and an arbitrary and conventional view of truth when he says that the 'first truths were arbitrarily made by those that first of all imposed names upon things, or received them from the impositions of others' (*Co* 3.36). Hobbes also says in the same work that definitions are 'principles of demonstration, being truths constituted arbitrarily by the inventors of speech, and therefore not to be demonstrated' (*Co* 3.37). In these cases, truth is clearly based upon an arbitrary convention among speakers.

In other passages suggesting a conventional view of truth, however, Hobbes does not explicitly say that truth is an arbitrary matter. 'To know truth', Hobbes says in *De Cive*, is 'the same thing as to remember that it was made by ourselves by the very usurpation of the words' (*EW* 2.304). In a different passage, Hobbes implies an arbitrary and conventional view of truth when he claims that 'falsity' results from using words in a manner that differs from their established meaning:

> This kind of error only deserves the name of *falsity*, as arising not from sense, nor from the things themselves, but from pronouncing rashly; for names have their constitution, not from the species of things, but from the will and consent of men. And hence it comes to pass, that men pronounce falsely, by their own negligence, in departing from such appellations as are agreed upon, and are not deceived neither by the things, nor by the

sense; for they do not perceive that the thing they see is called sun, but they give it that name from their own will and agreement. (*Co* 5.56)

In these cases, although Hobbes does not use the word 'arbitrary', the notion that we make truth 'from our will' implies that it is an arbitrary act, especially when one takes into consideration the passages explicitly stating the arbitrary character of name assignment.

Further evidence for the attribution of the conventional view of truth to Hobbes lies in the fact that it is supported by his explicit adherence to nominalism. According to Hobbes's nominalism, as we have seen, common names do not refer to objective similarities between objects, nor do they refer to genuinely existing universal essences. Nominalism, therefore, supports the conventional view of truth insofar as nominalism denies an objective basis for the assignment of names. If there are no objective similarities between things, then universal names are not assigned on the basis of objective features, thereby suggesting it is an entirely subjective and arbitrary matter. One could likewise argue for the attribution of nominalism to Hobbes on the basis that it is supported by his explicitly stated conventional view of truth. This view of truth supports nominalism because it claims that names are given to things by the will, and not on account of any objective similarities. The two views, then, are so closely linked together that evidence for one often provides evidence for the other.

5.2.b The Correspondence Theory of Truth

Despite the explicit endorsement of a conventional view of truth, there is plenty of evidence for ascribing a correspondence view of truth to Hobbes. In his *Anatomy of Leviathan*, F. S. McNeilly defends the view that Hobbes adheres to a more traditional view of truth in which propositions are made true on account of a relationship between propositions and the 'nature of things'.[19] McNeilly suggests that Hobbes venerates geometry on account of its ability to demonstrate truths about the world from a 'set of first principles which were certain but non-tautologous'.[20] Evidence for his interpretation is found in *De Corpore*, wherein Hobbes apparently advances a 'self-evidence theory of mathematics' that involves a 'process of logical deduction from a set of first principles which are known by themselves'.[21] According to McNeilly, *De Corpore* makes two important statements about the characteristics of primary propositions in geometry, namely, that they are (1) 'explications' of the 'nature of things' and (2) not 'matters for arbitrary decision'.[22] McNeilly offers two pieces of evidence for his interpretation, the first of which is Hobbes's definitions of place and motion:

> For example, he that has a true conception of place, cannot be ignorant of this definition, *place is that space which is possessed or filled adequately by some body*; and so, he that conceives *motion* aright, cannot but know that *motion is the privation of one place, and the acquisition of another.* (Co 6.70)

The truth of these definitions, in McNeilly's opinion, relies upon their ability to reveal the 'natures' of place and motion:

> Thus it is not just a matter of deciding how a word is to be used, but of conceiving of something *correctly*. And there is something which someone who conceives correctly cannot be ignorant of: but if he cannot be ignorant of it he must *know* it. Therefore those definitions which are primary propositions do not on this view express linguistic decisions but embody some fundamental knowledge about the nature of the world.[23]

To 'know' a definition is true, according to McNeilly, one must have a 'correct' conception. In addition, to have a 'correct' conception is to have a conception that accurately embodies 'knowledge about the nature of the world'.

In the second case, McNeilly argues against the conventional interpretation by appealing to the fact that Hobbes says primary propositions are 'known to themselves' and 'known to nature'.[24] If the conventional interpretation accurately describes Hobbes's position, McNeilly contends, the veracity of primary propositions would hinge upon the truth of an arbitrary definition. This, however, seems to clash with the view that primary propositions are 'known to nature', a phrase that McNeilly equates with 'known through itself' and 'manifest of itself'. The primary proposition concerning motion, in other words, would not be known through itself, but it would be contingent upon an arbitrary and conventional definition. As McNeilly says: 'Since he [Hobbes] has just been arguing that demonstration proceeds from definitions, a proposition that can be demonstrated *from* a definition is precisely not what he intends by "first principle," which is a definition which cannot be derived from a definition.'[25] According to McNeilly's interpretation, then, primary principles correctly describe non-linguistic facts about the world and they are not conventional or arbitrary.

Although McNeilly interprets Hobbes's view of truth as a correspondence theory, he recognizes the obvious fact that Hobbes often speaks of truth in terms of conventional and arbitrary agreement. For this reason, McNeilly accuses Hobbes of a blatant contradiction: '[In] *De Corpore* different accounts [of truth] were given, in flat contradiction of each other.'[26] A careful look at the evidence, however, reveals that Hobbes's position on truth is more consistent than McNeilly leads us to believe. Recall that when Hobbes speaks explicitly about truth in this work, he clearly endorses a conventional view. Although a correspondence theory of truth might be suggested by some of Hobbes's statements, I suggest that McNeilly's evidence is still consistent with the conventional interpretation.

The first piece of evidence for McNeilly's interpretation, as we have seen, is Hobbes's definitions of motion and place. According to McNeilly, Hobbes thinks that to have a true conception of motion or place is to 'know' (or 'not be ignorant of') a particular fact about the world. The passage quoted by McNeilly, however, does not require such an interpretation. I present the passage again for the sake of clarity.

> [H]e that has a true conception of place, cannot be ignorant of this definition, *place is that space which is possessed or filled adequately by some body*; and so, he that conceives *motion* aright, cannot but know that *motion is the privation of one place, and the acquisition of another.* (*Co* 6.70)

Hobbes's claim that one 'knows' what motion is, in other words, is perfectly consistent with the claim that one 'is not ignorant' of an arbitrary and conventional definition. As we have already seen, to speak falsely is to depart from conventional appellations: 'men pronounce falsely, by their own negligence, in departing from such appellations as are agreed upon' (*Co* 5.56). To speak truly, one must use accepted names and definitions. In this way, someone who has a true conception of place 'must not be ignorant' of the accepted and conventional definition.

McNeilly's second piece of evidence, although relatively more convincing, does not necessarily provide support for his interpretation. According to McNeilly, propositions that are 'known to nature' may be equated with 'known through itself'. Both of the terms are understood by McNeilly to imply that they cannot be conventional. In this case, I believe McNeilly misunderstands what Hobbes means by 'known to nature.' To see why, it is instructive to first recognize that propositions 'known to nature' are acquired by an act of reason.

> And this is the meaning of that common saying, namely that some things are more known to us, others more known to

nature; for I do not think that they, which so distinguish, mean that something is known to nature, which is known to no man; and therefore, by those things we take notice of by our senses, and, by more known to nature, those we acquire the knowledge of by reason. (*Co* 6.67)

To say something is 'known to nature', for Hobbes, is not to say that it is intuitively obvious or self-evident, but that it is *acquired* through an act of reason. This does not necessarily mean, as McNeilly claims, that primary principles are 'explications of the nature of the world' or that they are 'not matters for arbitrary decision'.

The best evidence McNeilly presents for his interpretation is Hobbes's description of primary principles as 'manifest of themselves' (*Co* 6.69). For McNeilly, to say primary propositions are manifest of themselves is to say an understanding of them does not rely upon definitions of other terms. This raises a very interesting problem for Hobbes, which will be made clear through an example. According to Hobbes, '*motion is the privation of one place, and the acquisition of another*' (*Co* 6.70). If McNeilly's interpretation is correct, then this definition of motion would not rely upon other definitions. The problem with this view is that the knowledge of the definition of motion requires knowledge of the other terms in the definition. To know that motion is the *privation of one place and the acquisition of another*, is it not necessary to know the definitions of 'privation', 'place', and 'acquisition'? How can I know that motion is a kind of privation without knowing what privation means? It seems that it would be impossible to know a primary principle without knowing the definitions of the terms within the principle itself. According to McNeilly, if a primary proposition is manifest of itself, then the proposition is not arbitrary and conventional. A more reasonable interpretation is that 'manifest of itself' means that it is obviously true to a person who understands the arbitrary definitions of the terms that make up the primary principle.

If I am correct, then McNeilly's evidence does not provide adequate support for the conclusion that Hobbes's primary principles reveal truths about the nature of the world and thus does not support the conclusion that Hobbes ascribes to a correspondence theory of truth. Before we put this issue behind us, however, we should examine more evidence for attributing a correspondence notion of truth to Hobbes. In his book, *Thomas Hobbes and the Science of Moral Virtue*, David Boonin-Vail interprets Hobbes as an adherent of a correspondence view of truth. In reference to Hobbes's geometry, Boonin-Vail claims the 'idea that geometrical definitions are purely arbitrary constructs' is 'alien to Hobbes's conception of geometry'.[27] Although Boonin-Vail specifically criticizes the interpretation of an arbitrary notion of truth, his evidence is applicable to the conventional interpretation as well. Boonin-Vail, like McNeilly, refers to Hobbes's definitions of place and motion as evidence for this claim.

Boonin-Vail provides support for McNeilly's interpretation in *Thomas Hobbes and the Science of Moral Virtue*.[28] Boonin-Vail, however, presents additional evidence that strongly suggests a correspondence view. In one place, Hobbes proclaims that mathematical definitions 'must not only be true, but likewise accurate' (*PPG* 113). To 'define well', Hobbes continues, is to 'circumscribe with Words the Things in Hand, and that clearly, and with as much Bevity as can be, that no ambiguity be left, is a very difficult Task, and not so much a Work of Art, as of the natural intellect' (*PPG* 113). The 'nature of a definition', Hobbes claims in a different text, 'consists in this, that it exhibits a clear idea of the thing defined' (*Co* 6.84). These passages suggest, as Boonin-Vail points out, that definitions are 'fixed by the nature of the thing in hand'.[29] Boonin-Vail concludes that 'definitions can be clear or unclear, better or worse, right or wrong, true or false, depending upon how well they correspond to the phenomenon they attempt to describe, and Hobbes does not hesitate to speak of definitions in this way'.[30] For Boonin-Vail, this viewpoint is 'clearly revealed in one of the extremely rare displays of humility in Hobbes's writings'.[31] Boonin-Vail is here referring to Hobbes's admission that a previously given definition of parallel lines was 'not, as it stands, universally true' (*SL* 254). Since Hobbes admits his definition is wrong, Boonin-Vail says, the definition 'cannot simply be stipulated, for in that case there can be no such mistake for the author of a definition to make'.[32]

The evidence presented by Boonin-Vail supports the view that Hobbes does not consistently adhere to his conventional view of truth, at least in regard to certain geometric propositions. The truth of such propositions, in other words, is not simply a matter of knowing a conventional definition, but it is a matter of discovering some 'fixed nature' of geometrical objects. Because of these cases, I believe, Hobbes's view of truth is genuinely inconsistent. If we turn to a discussion of 'truth' in his political philosophy, we shall find further evidence for Hobbes's adherence to a correspondence view of truth. Hobbes, as discussed in Chapter 2, believes his political philosophy provides a solution to the problem of ideological warfare precisely because it is supposed to be grounded upon a 'true' and 'indisputable' foundation. It seems to be a necessary requirement for the success of Hobbes's science of virtue and vice that the truth of its principles is not simply a matter of conventional agreement. Political conflict, as we have seen, is often caused by ideological disputes that frequently lead to real warfare. Hobbes's science of virtue and vice is supposed to settle such disputes by proving the necessity of an absolute sovereign power. As long as Hobbes's opponents remain firmly committed to their seditious opinions, no amount of force can change their minds. It is necessary, in other words, to prove to them that their opinions are wrong and need to be altered to attain a state of peace. In Hobbes's opinion, geometry provides the methodological model for his political science because of its ability to unify conflicting opinions on the basis of 'indisputable' principles. Political philosophy, like geometry, must begin from indisputable principles to prove the truth of its conclusions. If the primary principles, however, are simply a matter of agreement, then political philosophy would not succeed because there would be no objective conditions that make such principles 'indisputable'.

It must now be questioned whether Hobbes believes his primary principles of political philosophy are true in a conventional or a correspondence sense. It seems that the success of Hobbes's political philosophy requires that the principles be true in the sense that they correspond to or describe essential characteristics of humans. If the primary principles are to be 'indisputable', then agreement to them requires an objective foundation in the nature of things. If such principles are true simply by agreement, then Hobbes does not provide a reason for agreeing to these principles in the first place. A number of scholars have already recognized this point. Jean Hampton, for example, claims that 'Hobbes writing *Leviathan* proves he rejects that moral truths could only be conventional.'[33] In the words of Robert Russell, 'Hobbes never for a moment regarded his own demonstrations as a mere matter of word juggling, and was firmly convinced that his deductions led to the very heart of reality.'[34] Briefly put, Hobbes does not wholeheartedly adhere to a conventional view of truth in his political philosophy since he believes his principles of human nature are true in the traditional sense of correspondence.

5.3 The Political Influence as Explanation

How shall we explain these obvious inconsistencies in Hobbes's view of truth? Scholars are usually left scratching their heads wondering how to do so. Robert Russell, for example, finds no explanation for the 'curious' inconsistencies:

Whatever be the explanation of these curious passages [claiming truth is conventional], this much remains certain: that Hobbes in the exposition of his philosophy often relinquishes this *quasi* verbal truth and falsehood, and regards truth in the traditional sense, as being essentially a relation between thing and thought.[35]

The explicit endorsement of a conventional view of truth, therefore, is seen as 'curious' because there seems to be no reason for Hobbes to accept such a view. John Danford, as well, claims it is a 'picture that is curious in several respects' and that 'Hobbes never satisfactorily resolves this problem [of inconsistent notions of truth]'.[36] McNeilly, as we have seen, accuses Hobbes of an obvious contradiction. Most commentators simply claim that Hobbes is careless and has not adequately addressed the issues.

I suggest that the inconsistencies in Hobbes's view of truth indicate a political influence operating within his natural philosophy. The basic idea of my suggestion is that there is a pattern of political influence that leads Hobbes to *accept* specific positions in natural philosophy that he has good scientific or logical reasons to *reject*. In this case, Hobbes has political reasons for adopting the conventional view of truth, although he has philosophical reasons to reject it. The theoretical tensions in his natural philosophy have their origin in incompatible aims of Hobbes's political and natural philosophy. On the one hand, Hobbes tries to prove the necessity of an absolute political sovereign who is the final arbiter on all matters, to the point where the sovereign decides what is true and false. On the other hand, Hobbes contends his natural philosophy is true on its own merits, that it is a 'science'. Hobbes's philosophy, in this instance, embodies the problem faced by relativists who try to establish the relativity of all views, except for their own. If Hobbes's political ideas influence his natural philosophy, at least in the ways discussed, then the inconsistencies are not curious at all. Instead, given Hobbes's political ideas, I argue, such inconsistencies are inevitable.

The first point to establish, then, is that the conventional view of truth provides theoretical support for Hobbes's political absolutism. As previously mentioned, Hobbes believes civil disorder is caused, in part, by ideological conflicts over religion, morality and politics.[37] The solution to such problems is the creation of a sovereign power that will, in a real sense, determine the definitions of certain controversial words through the drafting of civil laws.

> All controversies are bred from hence, that the opinions of men differ concerning *meum* and *teum*, *just* and *unjust*, *profitable* and *unprofitable*, *good* and *evil*, *honest* and *dishonest*, and the like; which every man esteems according to his own judgment: it belongs to the same chief power to make some common rules for men, and to declare them publicly, by which every man may know what may be called his, what another's, what good, what evil. (*Ci* 6.178)

The sovereign, in other words, is responsible for determining the 'truth' about justice, goodness, the law, and other such moral and legal concepts. To know the truth about justice, to put it another way, one must know what the civil sovereign means by 'justice'. The conventional view of truth therefore provides epistemological support for Hobbes's political solution.

Given the conceptual connection between the conventional view of truth and Hobbes's political solution, I suggest that political ideas are partially responsible for the acceptance of the conventional view of truth. Given his belief that verbal disputes over the 'truth of the matter' often lead to conflict, this view of truth would be a reasonable one for him to adopt. But what are the reasons for him to reject it? As many scholars suggest, Hobbes does not strictly adhere to this position partly because he believes his own philosophy is true in a non-conventional sense. For the sake of the truth of his own natural philosophy, then, Hobbes has a good reason to reject the conventional view of truth. If it is the case, as it seems, that Hobbes is trying to establish a demonstrable science on the basis of *indisputable* principles, then why does he explicitly endorse a conventional view of truth? My answer is that Hobbes's goal of defending political absolutism leads him to explicitly endorse a view that he has good scientific reasons to reject. Or, to put it in general terms, a political influence operates within Hobbes's natural philosophy leading him to accept an opinion, for political purposes, that is in tension with his scientific and 'strictly philosophical' goals.

5.4 Conclusion

The thesis that a political influence is responsible for the inconsistencies in Hobbes's theory of truth provides a reasonable explanation that fits the textual evidence. Nevertheless, I must still offer a defence against possible objections and I must also consider the legitimacy of alternative views. Part of my defence is that there is a pattern of a political influence, a systematic penetration that is seen throughout Hobbes's natural philosophy. Thus, my position becomes stronger the more a political influence is revealed. In the next two chapters, I will further reveal the political influence and the manner in which it leads to inconsistencies in Hobbes's philosophy. I will address possible objections and alternative views in the final chapter.

Notes

1. Watkins, J. (1965), *Hobbes's System of Ideas*. London: Hutchinson & Co., p. 99.
2. Ibid.
3. Goldsmith, M. M. (1966), *Hobbes's Science of Politics*. New York: Columbia University Press, p. 2.
4. Soles, D. H. (1996), *Wits and Spider Webs: A Study in Hobbes's Philosophy of Language*. Aldershot: Ashgate Publishing, p. 1.
5. Danford, J. (1980), 'The Problem of Language in Hobbes's Political Science', *Journal of Politics*, 42, 102.
6. Whelan, F. (1981), 'Language and Its Abuses in Hobbes's Political Philosophy', *American Political Science Review*, 75, 60.
7. Ibid., p. 59.

8. Ibid., p. 60.
9. See Lynch, W. T. (1991), 'Politics in Hobbes's Mechanics: The Social as Enabling', *Studies in the History of the Philosophy of Science*, 22 (2), 295–320.
10. See Section 3.3.
11. John Watkins points out that his earlier and 'mistaken' opinion on this topic was that a 'name is the name of something in the mind'. By advocating this interpretation, he claims he 'made this mistake in good company' since this is the view of Hobbes held by both J. S. Mill and M. J. Oakeshott. See Watkins, *Hobbes's System of Ideas*, p. 101.
12. Ibid., p. 102.
13. Isabel Hungerland and George Vick argue that Hobbes's theory of signification involves much more than a two-term correlation between names and world/conception. See Hungerland, I. and Vick, G. (1981), 'Hobbes's Theory of Language, Speech, and Reasoning', in Hobbes, T., *Thomas Hobbes: Part I of De Corpore*. Aloysius Martinich (trans.). New York: Abaris. According to Hungerland and Vick, a name, properly speaking, does not signify anything when it is spoken in isolation. Instead, signifying occurs only in propositional form, when speakers intend to communicate their wishes, desires, beliefs, and so on, to others. If, for example, an individual says the word 'stone', the word may be used to refer either to a conception in the mind or to an actual object, but the individual is not really signifying anything. Communication requires propositions: 'the proposition is the unit of communication, that we do not signify, communicate our beliefs, and so on, by uttering words in isolation. Accordingly, explanations of the signification of words must refer us to the role they can play in complete communications' (p. 58). For this reason, Hungerland and Vick do not use 'signify' to refer to a 'name–conception' relationship, as if each individual word signifies one conception. Hobbes's theory of signification is deeper and richer than normally thought because it involves more than a theory about a two-term correlating relationship. Thus, when Hungerland and Vick speak about either the 'name–thing' or the 'name–conception' relationship, they employ such terms as 'denote', 'name', 'apply to' and 'refer to'. Hobbes, it is said, 'is able to escape confusing (as so many have done) signifying and signification (or meaning) with a relation between words and things – that is, with denoting, referring, applying to, or naming' (p. 102).
14. Watkins, *Hobbes's System of Ideas*, p. 102.
15. Soles, *Strong Wits and Spider Webs*, p. 61.
16. Ibid., p. 68.

17. Ibid., p. 69.
18. Hungerland and Vick, 'Hobbes's Theory of Language, Speech, and Reasoning', p. 23.
19. McNeilly, F. S. (1968), *The Anatomy of Leviathan*. London: St Martin's Press.
20. McNeilly, *The Anatomy of Leviathan*, p. 63.
21. Ibid., p. 62.
22. Ibid.
23. Ibid.
24. Ibid., p. 63.
25. Ibid.
26. Ibid., p. 88.
27. Boonin-Vail, D. (1994), *Thomas Hobbes and the Science of Moral Virtue*. Cambridge: Cambridge University Press, p. 31.
28. Ibid.
29. Ibid.
30. Ibid.
31. Ibid., p. 32.
32. Ibid.
33. Hampton, J. (1986), *Hobbes and the Social Contract Tradition*. Cambridge: Cambridge University Press, p. 30.
34. Russell, R. (1939), *Natural Law in the Philosophy Thomas Hobbes*, Dissertation for the Doctorate in the Faculty of Philosophy of the Pontifical Gregorian University, p. 15.
35. Ibid.
36. Danford, 'The Problem of Language in Hobbes's Political Science', 112.
37. See Section 3.1

6

The Politics of Nominalism

6.0 Introduction

In the previous chapter, I suggested that inconsistencies in Hobbes's view of truth result from a political influence in his natural philosophy. I also suggested that this is one example of a pattern of influence that encourages Hobbes to *accept* specific positions in natural philosophy that he has good scientific or logical reasons to *reject*. In this chapter, I present further evidence for my position. Contrary to the traditional interpretation of influence, once again, I will point out that Hobbes's discussion of universals is not a topic 'far removed' from political matters. In fact, as with his theory of truth and his philosophy of mind, there are important political implications lurking in this topic of natural philosophy. In addition, as with his theory of truth, the inconsistencies in his view of universals may be explained by appealing to a political influence. Hobbes, as we shall see, has political reasons to accept a nominalist view of universals even though he has strong philosophical reasons to reject it. In Section 6.1, I discuss Hobbes's nominalist view of universals. The inconsistencies of his position are then treated in Section 6.2. I will suggest, in Section 6.3., that the thesis of a political influence provides a strong explanation for these inconsistencies.

6.1 Hobbes's Nominalism

Nominalism in Hobbes's philosophy involves both an ontological claim about the existence of universal essences and a linguistic claim about the role of universal names. Nominalism is best explained by contrasting it with the positions of realism and conceptualism. Realism claims universal names refer to real essences that exist in the world. A primary reason to accept realism is to explain the apparent fact that particular things share common qualities or stand in certain relationships to each other. Two white objects, for example, appear to share the common property *white*, a property that exists in a genuine sense and is referred to by the name 'white'. Such commonalities include relationships, such as 'to the left of'. If A is to the left of B, and X is to the left of Y, then the relationship between A and B is the same as the relationship between X and Y. Particular things, in other words, may share a common relationship, just as they share a common property. The realist, then, makes the ontological claim that common properties or relations genuinely exist. In addition, the realist asserts that the role of universal names is to refer to universal things. Realists are generally divided into two types, depending upon whether the properties or relations are said to exist independently of particulars (Platonism) or exist within particulars (Aristotelianism). In both cases, however, the fundamental ontological claim of the realist is that universals exist.

The denial of real universal essences is sometimes seen as sufficient to label a philosopher a nominalist.[1] This denial, however, is not necessarily indicative of nominalism. Conceptualism, a position related to nominalism, also denies the realist claim that universal names refer to real essences. The conceptualist however, unlike the nominalist, contends that universal names refer to mental conceptions that have been constructed through a process of abstracting common qualities. So, for example, the term 'horse', according to conceptualism, refers to a concept in the mind, a concept fabricated by abstracting common qualities from the appearances of various horses. The conceptualist denies the existence of real essences and affirms the presence of a mental essence or concept, which is referred to by a common term. The nominalist, by contrast, denies even the existence of universal concepts. A universal name, in this case, does not refer to anything universal, but it is simply a name. The 'distinction between conceptualism and nominalism', as Richard Aaron points out, 'must finally lie in this, that the former asserts the existence of a concept along with a name, whereas the latter denies the need for the concept and holds that the universal is merely a name'.[2] In this description of the distinction between nominalism, realism and conceptualism, the ontological and linguistic claims of the nominalist are revealed. With regard to ontology, the nominalist denies the existence of both real and nominal essences. In addition, the nominalist makes the linguistic claim that universal names are really just names of names.

The basic tenets of Hobbes's nominalism are discernible in his rejection of both realism and conceptualism. The rejection of realism is evidenced in the following passage, within which Hobbes claims some philosophers mistakenly assume that a universal name is the name of a real thing, separate from the individuals named by it.

> This universality of one name to many things hath been the cause that men think that the things themselves are universal. And do seriously contend, that besides Peter and John, and all the rest of the men that are, have been, or shall be in the world, there is yet someone else that we call man, viz., man in general, deceiving themselves by taking the universal, or the general appellation, for the thing it signifieth. (*El* 5.20)

Hobbes also explicitly rejects conceptualism when he claims philosophers are mistaken who 'say the idea of anything is universal; as if there could be in the mind an image of a man, which were not the image of some one man, but a man simply, which is impossible; for every idea is one, and of one thing' (*Co* 5.60). A universal name, for Hobbes, does not refer to any genuinely existing thing (realism) or to a universal idea in the mind (conceptualism):

This word *universal* is never the name of anything existent in nature, nor of any idea or phantasm formed in the mind, but always the name of some word or name; so that when a *living creature*, a *stone*, or a *spirit*, or any other thing, is said to be *universal*, it is not to be understood that any man, stone, &c. ever was or can be universal, but only that these words, *living creature*, *stone*, &c. are *universal names*, that is names common to many things. (*Co* 2.20)

On the basis of such passages, then, one could reasonably conclude that Hobbes rejects both the realist and conceptualist accounts of universals.

6.2 Inconsistencies in Hobbes's Account of Universals

In *Hobbes's System of Ideas*, John Watkins clearly and thoroughly discusses an inconsistency in Hobbes's view of universals. According to Watkins, nominalism is inconsistent with a number of passages that admit 'similitudes' between things.[3] In *Leviathan*, for example, Hobbes says 'one universal name is imposed on many things, for their similitude in some quality, or other accident' (*L* 4.103). This passage reveals that Hobbes, as Watkins says, 'not only admitted resemblances between things, but resemblances with respect to certain properties or accidents; and he said, in effect, that a common name gets extended to new objects not arbitrarily, but in accordance with such objective resemblances'.[4] The problem is that the recognition of common qualities seems to be inconsistent with the claim that everything named is individual and singular.' If, for example, the common name 'white' is applied to two objects, it seems they have the same property. If the *same* property exists in two separate things, however, then the name 'white' would signify two separate things. This poses a problem because, according to nominalism, everything named is individual. On account of this, Watkins 'can see no escape from the conclusion that [Hobbes's] statement that some names are names of accidents is inconsistent with his statement that there is nothing in the world universal but names, everything named being individual and singular'.[5] Echoing this view, Aaron claims the following:

> In intention, it seems clear, Hobbes was a nominalist in the narrow sense of the term. Whether he was consistently a nominalist is another matter, for, in the same chapter of Leviathan, to look no farther, what he says about the universal triangle seems hardly consonant with strict nominalism.[6]

If these scholars are correct, then Hobbes's explicit adherence to nominalism is betrayed by his implied ontology of accidents and properties.

Traditionally, most Hobbes scholars accuse him of inconsistency on this matter.[7] According to Hungerland and Vick, for example, Hobbes's 'writings on this topic are sketchy, scattered throughout *De Corpore*, and at times extremely careless. Also in two crucial passages, the English translation, which Hobbes approved, is badly bungled'.[8] Hobbes, they say, also allowed his 'rhetoric to run away with him when he dealt with such topics – like nominalism – on which he felt strongly'.[9] In a recent article, however, G. K. Callaghan defends Hobbes against the accusation. Callaghan suggests that Hobbes be interpreted as an adherent of a 'particularist' theory of accidents, which 'treats accidents as a special category of particulars'.[10] According to particularism, to say accidents are particulars is to say they are completely determinate. As Callaghan points out, the theory holds that a colour, for example, is always of some determinate hue and shade. In addition, such a theory is committed to the 'thesis that an accident can belong to no more than one particular object'.[11] The 'white' of object X, according to this thesis, is not identical to the 'white' of object Y. In this case, 'white' is used as a common name to refer to the two individual objects (taken individually) because they *resemble* each other with regard to colour. Resemblance of accidents, then, is not to be equated with the identity of accidents. Since particularism holds that the names of accidents are the names of determinate particulars, it is perfectly consistent with both the linguistic and ontological claims of nominalism. According to Callaghan, then, particularism offers Hobbes the only means of escaping the inconsistency under investigation: 'Hobbes is committed to particularism on pain of inconsistency with the general dictum that only names are universal.'[12]

The question, then, is whether we should attribute particularism to Hobbes to help him avoid being inconsistent. Although there is no direct proof that Hobbes explicitly adopts such a position, Callaghan provides a fair amount of indirect evidence. The basis of this evidence consists of two points: (1) particularism is the only view of accidents that is consistent with Hobbes's nominalism and (2) when Hobbes discusses accidents themselves, he says nothing inconsistent with particularism. Given Hobbes's nominalist claim that everything that is named is individual, I see no way to dispute the first point. To evaluate the second point, however, we need to look more closely at what Hobbes says about accidents.

Hobbes's definition of accidents arises within the context of his discussion of the distinction between abstract and concrete names. A concrete name, Hobbes says, is the 'name of any thing which we suppose to have a being, and is therefore a subject' (*Co* 3.32). As examples of concrete names, Hobbes provides the following list: '*body, moveable, moved, figurate, a cubit high, hot, cold, like, equal, Appius, Lentulus*'. Included in this list are names that are usually considered qualities, e.g., *hot*. In this case, Hobbes is not saying that the word 'hot' signifies an existing thing, separated from a body that is hot. As Callaghan points out, such concrete names 'are not the names of qualities but, rather, common names for the members of different classes of concrete objects'.[13] 'Hot', in other words, is a concrete name that signifies one of the members of hot things. Abstract names, on the other hand, 'denote only the causes of concrete names, and not the things themselves' (*Co* 3.32). The following names are examples of abstract names: '*to be a body, to be movable, to be moved, to be figurate, to be of such quantity, to be hot, to be cold, to be like, to be equal, to be Appius, to be Lentulus*' (*Co* 3.32). According to Hobbes, an abstract name denotes a faculty or power in an object to cause those conceptions within us that most people would normally call the qualities of those objects:

> And these causes of names are the same with the causes of our conceptions, namely, some power of action, or affection of the thing conceived, which some call the manner by which any thing works upon our senses but by most men they are called *accidents*. (*Co* 3.32–3)

An accident, then, is a power of an object to create conceptions in us: '[T]hey answer best that define an *accident* to be the *manner by which any body is conceived*; which is all one as if they should say, an *accident is that faculty of any body, by which it works in us a conception of itself*' (*Co* 8.103). The function of accidents, according to this definition, is to provide a causal explanation of our conceptions of what are normally considered qualities.

Taking this function into account, Callaghan asserts that the accusation of inconsistency relies on an unwarranted assumption and that Hobbes's account of accidents is consistent with particularism:

> [A]ccidents furnish the causal basis for our recognition of similarities among concrete objects … The assumption that in order to grant accidents this function, Hobbes must have taken them for a species of universals is unwarranted. Hobbes is free to maintain that accidents are abstract particulars, different ranges of which bear resemblance relations to one another primitively.[14]

In addition, Callaghan refers to Hobbes's theory of propositions to reinforce his particularist interpretation:

According to Hobbes's theory of propositions, copulating the name of an accident (i.e., an abstract name) with the name of a name (i.e., a name of 'second intention') always results in a false proposition. By way of example, Hobbes speaks of the error that arises from saying that '*whiteness*, or some other accident, is a *genus* or *universal name*.' According to Hobbes, the error consists in the fact that 'not whiteness itself, but the word whiteness, is a genus, or a universal name'. (*Co* 6.60)

For Hobbes, then, such terms as 'genus' and 'universal' are not properly applied to accidents.[15] According to Callaghan, Hobbes strongly implies that universal names do not signify accidents themselves, although they may signify the names of accidents. Nothing in this account prohibits Hobbes from particularism. If this is correct, then, Hobbes's account of accidents is more consistent with nominalism than traditionally held.

Callaghan's argument is quite persuasive, although it is not entirely convincing. With regard to the two major points, I agree with Callaghan. In the first case, I accept Callaghan's point that particularism is the only view of accidents that is consistent with nominalism. I also agree with the second point that Hobbes, when he speaks explicitly about accidents themselves, does not say anything inconsistent with particularism. The problem arises, however, when Hobbes gives examples of accidents. As previously mentioned, Hobbes says that 'one universal name is imposed on many things, for their similitude in some quality, or other accident' (*L* 4.103). Now, in some examples of 'similitudes', his account is consistent with particularism, but in other examples it is not. With regard to two objects being white, for instance, it is perfectly legitimate to say that Hobbes *could* hold the opinion that each instance of 'white' is a determinate particular. After all, he does say two objects are given one universal name on the basis of a 'similitude', which is closer to the meaning of 'similarity' than 'identity'. Yet, when Hobbes speaks of other types of objects, e.g., mathematical objects, it becomes virtually impossible to deny a relation of identity. An example of this is found in a passage that I examined in Chapter 5. In this passage, Hobbes's main point is to show how language is necessary for scientific knowledge. If a 'man that hath not the use of speech', Hobbes says, 'set before his eyes a triangle and by it two right angles' then 'he may by meditation compare and find, that the three angles of that triangle, are equall to those two right angles that stand by it' (*L* 4.103). Putting aside an evaluation of the main point of this passage, it is clear that Hobbes's example is best interpreted as inconsistent with particularism. Here, Hobbes strongly suggests the *same* property is in all triangles. Could it be the case that Hobbes is saying that the 'equality with two right angles' that is shared by all triangles is simply a matter of similarity, and not identity? It is difficult to answer this question affirmatively since the notion of 'equality' is a relation of identity rather than similarity. Hobbes's example of the triangle implies that an identical quality exists in a number of different concrete individuals. The general point could be expanded and applied to qualitative relationships among all geometric figures. Since this is the case, Hobbes's example of shared qualities among geometric objects is inconsistent with the claim that everything named is a particular.

Hobbes's view of universals, then, is ultimately inconsistent. It should be noted that the inconsistency exists between an *explicit* account of universals and an *implied* notion of accidents. When Hobbes speaks explicitly about universals, in other words, he advocates nominalism, but in practice he does not abide by it. The rejection of nominalism is necessary, at least in the realm of geometry, for the knowledge of universal truths expounded in this science. As seen in the previous chapter, a similar tension between an explicit and an implicit account exists in Hobbes's view of truth.

6.3 The Political Influence as Explanation

Hobbes, I believe, accepts nominalism for political reasons, even though he has good scientific reasons to reject it. In this section, I discuss the political relevance of nominalism and suggest that its inconsistencies may be explained by the presence of a political influence. There are two ways in which nominalism is politically relevant. First, it is part and parcel of the rejection of Aristotelian metaphysics. As I mentioned in Chapter 3, Hobbes's metaphysical rebukes of Aristotle serve the political function of revealing the absurdities in the rhetoric of his political opponents. Nominalism may be used to perform the same fundamental task. According to Aristotle's realist view of universals, substantial forms existing within particular things provide these things with the essential characteristics of their species. To use such words as 'form', 'essence' and 'species' in reference to material things, according to Hobbes, is to employ a form of insignificant speech. Nominalism holds that such universals are simply the names of names, and so the Aristotelian use of them is insignificant. And since insignificant speech is politically dangerous, Hobbes's nominalism is politically relevant.

Second, nominalism is politically relevant because of its association with voluntarism, which is a theological view with important political implications. To explain voluntarism and its political implications, I will begin by discussing a theological debate in medieval scholasticism. The debate centres around a disagreement on the relationship between the *potentia absoluta* (absolute power) and the *potentia ordinata* (ordained power) of God. In his book *Capacity and Volition*, William Courtenay traces the history of the *potentia absoluta/ordinata* distinction.[16] Digging into the writings of Augustine, Courtenay discovers a primitive form that would evolve into the standard distinction by the thirteenth century. As he sees it, the distinction is one between 'capacity' and 'volition': 'between what God is theoretically able to do and what God actually wills to do'.[17] Augustine set the background for a discussion of God's power along these lines with such phrases as 'He could but did not wish to,' or 'He could have through power, but not through justice.'[18]

For Christian interpreters of the Bible, certain passages dealing with an apparent lack of God's power posed hermeneutical problems and Augustine's terminology provided a context for resolution. In the eleventh century, for example, Peter Damian grappled with a passage in the Bible in which God was said by Jerome to be unable to restore the virginity of a maiden. Damian, reluctant to accept such a restriction on God's power, had interpreted this passage as saying that God could not restore virginity because He did not wish to.[19] In this case, God has the capacity to restore the maiden's virginity, but not the volition. The distinction between what God is able to do and what God wishes to do was further developed by theologians in the eleventh and twelfth centuries. By 1245, Courtenay claims, the distinction had come to have a definite acceptation, what he calls the 'theological interpretation'. *Potentia absoluta* and *potentia ordinata* were not viewed as two separate powers of God, but they were one power seen from different perspectives. *Potentia absoluta* referred to the range of possibilities originally open to God at creation, i.e., a capacity rather than an act of will. *Potentia ordinata*, on the other hand, was considered the preordained will of God, i.e., God's power as volition.

In the late medieval period, Duns Scotus and Ockham endorsed the voluntaristic view that God's absolute power is not restricted in any fashion. In taking such a position, they answered the age-old philosophical question first expressed in Plato's *Euthyphro*. In his search for a definition of piety, Socrates asks Euthyphro whether the 'pious is loved by the gods because it is pious' or whether it is 'pious because it is loved by the gods'.[20] If we broaden the notion of piety to include the notion of the Good, the question is whether the gods are responsible for the creation of the Good, or whether they themselves recognize the inherent characteristics of the Good. To put this question most generally: is the will of the gods constrained by the strictures of morality or is morality a creation of the will of the gods? Rationalists, such as Aquinas, believed it was part of God's ordained plan to be directed by the Good; *potentia ordinata* operates within the confines established by the Good. Once this plan was established, *potentia absoluta* cannot extend beyond *potentia ordinata*. Voluntarists, on the other hand, believed that God's absolute power is not restricted in any fashion since the Good is itself created by the will of God.

Gordon Leff, in *The Dissolution of the Medieval Outlook*, points out the moral implications of voluntarism:

> It is arguable that Duns' doctrine of ethics was his most potent legacy to the later Middle Ages. For in making God's will the sole arbiter of good and bad by reference only to what he wills, Duns effectively subsumed ethics under logic and began to slide to ethical relativism: something is good because God wills it rather than it is willed because it is good.[21]

The implications of voluntarism, we should note, are not restricted to ethics. The political implications of voluntarism were made explicit in the thirteenth century when canon lawyers drew comparisons between God's power and papal power. According to Courtenay, canon lawyers transformed the *absoluta/ordinata* distinction in order to deny that the pope was subject to law, insisting instead that he followed the law under a self-imposed obligation. The canonists equated *potentia absoluta* with the ability to act outside of established law, whether the actor is God or the pope (or, eventually, any agent with absolute power). Ordained power, by contrast, was exemplified by lawful conduct. Duns Scotus helped solidify this new 'canonist' interpretation of the distinction. An intellectual agent, Scotus says, 'can act in conformity with the right law, and then it acts according to its ordered power', but 'it can act outside that law or contrary to it, and in this there is absolute power that exceeds ordered power'.[22]

Voluntarism provides obvious support for Hobbes's political ideas. As I mentioned in Chapter 2, Hobbes's political philosophy advances an absolutist conception of sovereign power, according to which the sovereign, who is the 'mortal God', maintains the prerogative to act outside of the established law, which is itself a product of the sovereign power. In our discussion of the historical context surrounding the publication of Hobbes's translation of Thucydides' history, it was shown that one of the central political issues of the time was whether King Charles had the right to operate outside the boundaries of the law. Voluntarism provides assistance to one of the main elements of Hobbes's political philosophy, i.e., political absolutism. In his works, Hobbes advances a voluntaristic and absolutist notion of the power of both God and sovereign:

> That which men make among themselves here by pacts and covenants, and call by the name of justice, and according whereunto men are accounted and termed rightly *just* or *unjust*, is not that by which God Almighty's actions are to be measured or called just ... That which he does, is made just by doing it; just, I say, in him, though not always just in us.[23]

Hobbes says, '[l]egitimate kings [as does God] therefore make the things they command just, by commanding them, and those they forbid, unjust, by forbidding them' (*Ci* 12.244–5). In this manner, the theological view of voluntarism is important to Hobbes's absolutist political doctrine.

The conceptual connection between nominalism and voluntarism remains to be shown. In *The Legitimacy of the Modern Age*, Hans Blumenberg explains how the denial of universals is at the heart of the voluntaristic conception of God's power.[24] Once again, the conceptual link between these positions must be established by a brief philosophical genealogy. In Platonic cosmology, the created world is fashioned after a divine plan of universals existing in the mind of the demiurge. Due to the fact that particular things partake in Ideal Forms, the creation itself cannot be considered a pure creation; rather, such a 'creation' of individuals is like an assembly-line manufacture of pre-made essences. Ockham's denial of universals, according to Blumenberg, increases God's power because the production of each particular existent follows no pattern:

> This conception of creation is not an incidental piece of doctrine of the Nominalist school but is connected to its philosophical center, to the denial of universals ... The concept of the *potentia absoluta*, however, implies that there is no limit to what is possible, and this renders meaningless the interpretation of the universal as the repetition of a universal. Creation is now supposed to mean that every entity comes into existence from nothing, in such a way that even in respect to its conceptual definition it was not there previously.[25]

The nominalist view of universals, in other words, reveals the highest form of God's absolute power because every individual is uniquely created and does not follow an established pattern set by Ideal Forms. This view is not only contrary to Plato's realism, but it is also contrary, as Blumenberg notes, to the 'Aristotelian distinction between definite essential form and individuality'.[26]

To see the connection between voluntarism and nominalism clearly, one must notice that the Good is an Ideal Form, or universal. Nominalism, by denying the existence of universals, denies the existence of a universal Good. Voluntarism is intricately related to nominalism insofar as the former claims God's will is not restricted by the Good or by any other universal notions. If there are no universal moral standards, in other words, then a creation *ex nihilo* implies that God's will is responsible for determining morality. At the creation, God's will is not restricted by any universal moral standards; it is not restricted by the Good; it is an absolute power in the highest sense. In relation to Hobbes's political philosophy, nominalism provides theoretical support because it implies that goodness, justice or other moral notions, are created by the wielder of absolute power. It might be objected, of course, that God's absolute power is responsible for establishing moral standards, and so the sovereign's power should be restricted by the divine law created by God. As we have seen, however, Hobbes believes God's will is unknown and that the divine law requires interpretation. Since many controversies arise from differing religious opinions, peace requires that the divine law be interpreted by the sovereign power. If it is the case, as Hobbes believes it is, that there are no moral universals, then morality itself must be established by an act of the sovereign's will. In this manner, nominalism provides support to Hobbes's political absolutism.

Hobbes, then, has clear political reasons to accept the philosophical position of nominalism. The ontological claim of nominalism that denies the existence of universals is linked with both theological and political absolutism. For this reason, Hobbes probably found it to be an appealing philosophical view to adopt. In addition, the linguistic claim of nominalism that universal names do not refer to existing universals supports the view that there are no universal moral standards and thereby supports Hobbes's political argument. On the other hand, Hobbes has a strong philosophical reason to reject it. Geometry, as we have seen, is the highest form of science for Hobbes. Yet, because it requires universal claims of identity, Hobbes has a good reason to reject nominalism. If this is the case, then why does he so explicitly and adamantly adhere to nominalism? My answer should be clear; he does this because his desire to support political absolutism leads him to accept and explicity endorse nominalism. The thesis of a political influence, in other words, provides a reasonable explanation for inconsistencies found in Hobbes's natural philosophy.

6.4 Conclusion

In this chapter and the previous two, I have slowly built a case to show that, at the very least, the 'strictly philosophical' ideas of Hobbes's natural philosophy provided in the early chapters of *Leviathan* are not 'far removed' from politics and are not simply 'preliminary' to the main political argument. Instead, these ideas of natural philosophy are inherently political and carry important implications. To say Hobbes's natural philosophy has political consequences, however, does not necessarily mean there is a political influence at work, although it does suggest that he has political reasons to accept certain philosophical positions. The thesis of a political influence becomes stronger, however, when we see a pattern in which Hobbes accepts certain positions even though he has philosophical or scientific reasons to reject them. Hobbes's view of truth and his view of universals provide two examples of this pattern. The final example will be provided in the next chapter wherein I discuss Hobbes's view of reason.

Notes

1. Aaron, R. (1967), *The Theory of Universals*. Oxford: Clarendon Press.
2. Ibid., p. 20.
3. Watkins, J. (1965), *Hobbes's System of Ideas*. London: Hutchinson & Co., p. 107.
4. Ibid.
5. Ibid.
6. Aaron, *The Theory of Universals*, p. 21.
7. It is interesting that no scholar, as far as I know, has argued that Hobbes is entirely consistent. Instead, it often occurs that any explanation offered is ultimately admitted to be insufficient in some manner. This is clearly seen in, for example, Peters, R. (1956), *Hobbes*. Harmondsworth: Penguin Books. With regard to Hobbes's view of accidents, Peters claims that many scholars 'have held that it was inconsistent with his nominalism; for it is often said that his account of names of accidents was simply a way of smuggling in the Aristotelian account of the *universal in re*' (p. 129). It is clear, as Peters notes, that this 'is quite contrary to what Hobbes intended

to do, [so] it is essential to get a clear view of what Hobbes was trying to do' (p. 129). Yet, after carefully analysing the problem in relation to Hobbes's view of abstract terms, Peters asks, 'is there not still a puzzle about the status of such terms?' (p. 131).

8. Hungerland, I. and Vick, G. (1981), 'Hobbes's Theory of Language, Speech and Reasoning', in Hobbes, T., *Thomas Hobbes: Part I of De Corpore*. A. Martinich (trans.). New York: Abaris, p. 74.

9. Ibid., p. 23. To be fair, it should be noted that Hungerland and Vick believe that the 'general outlines of a theory that is consistent and plausible and highly original can be made out if we gather together the relevant passages in the *De Corpore* and read them carefully, in the light of what has thus far been discovered in his theory of signifying and naming'. See Hungerland and Vick, 'Hobbes's Theory of Language', p. 74. Nevertheless, they admit there are inconsistencies in what Hobbes actually says, which are partly attributed to his carelessness.

10. Callaghan, G. K. (2001), 'Nominalism, Abstraction, and Generality in Hobbes', *History of Philosophy Quarterly*, 18, 41.

11. Ibid, pp. 41–2.

12. Ibid., p. 42.

13. Ibid., p. 39.

14. Ibid., p. 44.

15. Ibid., p. 42.

16. Courtenay, W. (1990), *Capacity and Volition: A History of the Distinction of Absolute and Ordained Power*. Bergamo: Pierluigi Lubrina.

17. Ibid., p. 29.

18. Quoted in ibid.

19. See ibid., p. 25.

20. Plato (1981), *Euthyphro*, in *Five Dialogues*. G. M. A. Grube (trans.). Indianapolis, IN: Hackett Publishing, p. 10a.

21. Leff, G. (1976), *The Dissolution of the Medieval Outlook: An Essay on Intellectual and Spiritual Change in the Fourteenth Century*. New York: New York University Press, p. 54.

22. Quoted in Adams, M. M. (1987), *William Ockham*. Notre Dame: University of Notre Dame Press, Vol. 2, p. 1552.

23. See also *L* 31.399–400; *Ci* 15.292.

24. Blumenberg, H. (1983), *The Legitimacy of the Modern Age*. R. Wallace (trans.). Cambridge, MA: MIT Press.

25. Ibid., p. 153.

26. Ibid.

7

The Politics of Reason

7.0 Introduction

In the previous two chapters, I suggested that certain inconsistencies in Hobbes's natural philosophy are the result of a political influence in his natural philosophy. In this chapter, I continue to support my thesis that Hobbes *accepts* specific positions in natural philosophy for political reasons that he has good scientific or logical reasons to *reject*. As we shall see, further evidence for my position may be found in Chapter 5 of *Leviathan*, entitled 'Of Reason and Science'. Hobbes, in this chapter of *Leviathan*, defines reasoning in terms of addition and subtraction, discusses the use and ends of reason, stresses the importance of definitions, describes error as a form of senseless speech, reveals the ways in which errors in speech and reasoning occur, defines science as a form of syllogistic demonstration, and distinguishes between scientific knowledge and prudence. Since these topics have already been adequately discussed in Chapter 2, my comments will focus on Hobbes's view of reason. As before, I will point out inconsistencies and suggest that the thesis of a political influence provides a strong explanation for them. The evidence I have presented suggests that the thesis of a political influence provides a *reasonable* explanation for certain inconsistencies in Hobbes's natural philosophy, but I have not defended the idea that it is the *best* explanation. After I present my view of the political influence in Hobbes's view of reason in Sections 7.1 and 7.2, I will conclude the present work by showing that my explanation is the best among the possible alternatives.

7.1 Hobbes's View of Reason and Its Inconsistencies

Hobbes begins Chapter 5 of *Leviathan* by describing human reasoning as a form of calculation. 'When a man Reasoneth,' Hobbes says, 'he does nothing else but conceive a summe totall, from *Addition* of parcels; or conceive a Remainder, from *Subtraction* of one summe from another' (*L* 5.110). As we have seen, Hobbes's *De Corpore* uses an example to clarify his calculating notion of reason.[1] According to this example, a person adds the ideas of 'body', 'animated' and 'rational' together to create the idea of 'man'. Hobbes's philosophy of language, as we have seen, contains a computational model of proposition construction according to which names are added together. For Hobbes, reason carries out such addition of names. In fact, as the above description suggests, he believes reason is involved whenever anything is added together with, or subtracted from, something else. Arithmeticians compute numbers to find sums, logicians compute names to create propositions and syllogisms, political writers compute 'Pactions, to find men's duties', and lawyers compute '*Lawes* and *facts*, to find what is *right* and *wrong*' (*L* 5.110). 'In summe,' Hobbes claims, 'in what matter soever there is place for *addition* and *subtraction*, there is also a place for *Reason*; and where these have no place, there *Reason* has nothing at all to do' (*L* 5.110–1).

After defining reason, Hobbes addresses the possibility that in exercising one's own reason, an individual could go badly astray. '[A]s in Arithmetique', Hobbes says, 'unpractised men must, and Professors themselves may often erre, and cast up false; so also in any other subject of Reasoning, the ablest, most attentive, and most practised men, may deceive themselves, and inferre False Conclusions' (*L* 5.111). The exercise of reason, in other words, does not guarantee correct results; it does not ensure that one's reason is 'right reason'. Hobbes then points out that nature has not bestowed on anyone an infallible faculty of reason. Individuals, in exercising their own natural reason, frequently are led to believe that their own reason has arrived at the correct conclusion. Nevertheless, mistakes in reasoning happen and some standard of right reasoning must therefore be created.

> Not but that Reason it selfe is always Right Reason, as well as Arithmetique is a certain and infallible Art: But no one mans Reason, nor the Reason of anyone number of men, makes the certaintie; no more than an account is therefore well cast up, because a great many men have unanimously approved it. And therefore, as when there is a controversy in an account, the parties must by their own accord, set up for right Reason, the Reason of some Arbitrator, or judge, to whose sentence they will both stand, or their controversie must either come to blows, or be undecided, for want of a Right Reason constituted by Nature. (*L* 5.111)

People who claim that their own reason 'should be taken for right Reason', Hobbes says, betray 'their want of right Reason, by the claym they lay to it' (*L* 5.112).

Hobbes's use of 'reason' and 'right reason', as Gregory Kavka points out, contains a certain amount of ambiguity.[2] According to Kavka, Hobbes describes reason as both a process and a faculty. Hobbes's definition of reason, for example, specifically describes it as a process; reason is 'nothing but *Reckoning*' (*L* 5.111). According to this definition, reason is not a faculty that reckons, but it is identified with the process of computation itself. At the same time, however, Hobbes claims his definition is concerned with reason 'when wee reckon it among the Faculties of the mind' (*L* 5.111). This ambiguity, I believe, is not indicative of any major problems in Hobbes's account of reason. In this particular case, it does seem to be the result of Hobbes's carelessness. In the remainder of Chapter 5 of *Leviathan*, Hobbes is more careful to distinguish between the process and the faculty. In other cases where he speaks of the process of reason, he uses 'reasoning' or 'ratiocination', and not 'reason'.[3] Thus, when I speak of 'right reason', I will be referring to a faculty, and not a process.

A more serious problem is created by Hobbes's failure to maintain the distinction between reason and right reason, a failure that leads to a genuine inconsistency. In chapter 5 of *Leviathan*, Hobbes claims that the reason of an arbiter is to be taken for right reason. Hobbes calls this view of reason into question in the *Elements of Law*:

> Now when a man reasoneth from principles that are found indubitable by experience, all deceptions of sense and equivocation of words avoided, the conclusion he maketh is said to be according to right reason; but when from his conclusion a man may, by good ratiocination, derive that which is contradictory to any evident truth whatsover, then he is said to have concluded against reason. (*El* 5.22)

Hobbes implies that what is to count for right reason does not depend upon an established authority, but upon indubitable empirical principles: the inconsistency between these two accounts is quite clear. In *Leviathan*, on the one hand, Hobbes claims that no individual is naturally capable of reasoning correctly; no individual possesses right reason naturally. In the *Elements of Law*, on the other hand, Hobbes says that individuals may discover and know foundational principles on the basis of their own natural faculties.

The fact that this inconsistency arises from the juxtaposition between passages in two different works is not enough to attribute it to a maturation of Hobbes's thought. The same difficulty arises within the text of *Leviathan* itself, though not so explicitly. After deducing the laws of nature in Chapter 15, Hobbes declares that his 'true Doctrine of the Lawes of Nature is the true Morall Philosophy' (*L* 15.216). The laws of nature, which are the main components of Hobbes's 'science of Vertue and Vice', are 'dictates of reason' (*L* 15.216). Hobbes does not refer to the laws of nature as the 'dictates of *right* reason'. Nevertheless, he certainly implies that the reasoning responsible for the discovery and derivation of the laws of nature is *right*. Since Hobbes claims the 'true doctrine of the Laws of Nature is the true Morall Philosophie' and that it is a 'science of Vertue and Vice', he clearly implies that his own reasoning about these matters is right (*L* 15.216).

As with his views on universals and truth, Hobbes's account of reason is inherently inconsistent. Unlike these other views, however, scholars have not spent a great deal of energy on addressing, explaining or resolving the inconsistencies in Hobbes's account of right reason.[4] The reason for this, I believe, is that this particular inconsistency is simply a symptom of the problems in Hobbes's philosophy of language. Hobbes, as we have seen, fluctuates between a conventional view of truth and a correspondence view of truth. The same fluctuation is revealed in Hobbes's account of right reason. On the one hand, Hobbes's notion that an individual's natural reason cannot be right says, in effect, that one cannot discover the truth by reason alone. Instead, an established authority determines the truth of the matter or, alternatively, what is according to right reason. On the other hand, Hobbes's claim that right reason is based on indubitable principles says, in effect, that an individual can discover true principles, if they reason properly. The truth of the matter is to be discovered by the person exercising right reason.

Once again, then, we have an inconsistency that requires explanation. The thesis of the political influence, I suggest, provides us with a good one. In the following section, I discuss the political relevance of Hobbes's view of reason and I indicate how such relevance supports the thesis of a political influence.

7.2 The Political Influence as Explanation

Before I discuss the particular political relevance of Hobbes's notion of reason, I would like to briefly point out the political rhetoric employed in Chapter 5 of *Leviathan*. Hobbes, while elaborating on his views of reason and science, does not hesitate to point out how people 'use names that signifie nothing; but are taken up and learned by rote from the Schooles, as *hypostatical, transubstantiation, consubstantiate, eternal-Now*, and the like canting of Schoolemen' (*L* 5.115). Trusting in the absurd speech of the scholastics, Hobbes claims, does not simply lead one into error, but possibly into danger. 'But they that trusting onely to the authority of books, follow the blind blindly,' Hobbes says, 'are like him that trusting to the false rules of the master offence, ventures presumptively upon an adversary, that either kills, or disgraces him' (*L* 5.117). Hobbes, then, is unrelenting in his attack on the absurd speech of the Aristotelians which, as I have already stated, should be understood in political terms.[5]

The specific political relevance of Hobbes's notion of reason is readily apparent, since it provides obvious support not only for his political absolutism, but also for his criticism of common law lawyers. In the first case, Hobbes uses the lack of a natural right reason to infer the necessity of an arbiter in cases of dispute. As we have seen, Hobbes frequently denies that individuals, by use of their own natural faculties, can certainly discover truth in any field of discourse. In Chapter 3, for example, I have shown that Hobbes is critical of the Presbyterian view that private conscience determines ethical values. Similarly, in the same chapter, I have shown that Hobbes finds Aristotle's doctrine of the mean insufficient because it allows individuals to determine ethical values. Hobbes's criticism of Descartes' 'light of nature', discussed in Chapter 4, revealed that individuals do not have an inner source of certainty. In all of these cases, Hobbes denies that individuals determine the 'truth' about things according to their own private judgment. As with the conventional view of truth, Hobbes's view of right reason contends there are no natural standards of truth, but that such standards must be created by an authority established by agreement. Since differences of opinions often result in genuine conflict, the best means of avoiding disputes is to establish an arbiter who will have the final say on these matters. In this manner, then, Hobbes's view of right reason provides support for his political absolutism.

The view of right reason may also be interpreted as a direct attack on the opinions of common law lawyers. In the historical investigation of the circumstances surrounding the Petition of Right, it was shown that common law lawyers believed King Charles I was subject to the common law.[6] At this point, we should recall that the student in Hobbes's dialogue on the common laws attributes the following view to Sir Edward Coke.

[I]f all the reason that is dispersed into so many heads, were united into one, yet he [i.e., the King] could not make such a law as a law of England is, because by many successions of ages it hath been fined and refined by an infinite number of grave and learned men. And this it is, he [i.e., Coke] calls common law. (*D* 14)

The common law lawyers, according to the student, claim this 'legal reason is *summa ratio*' and '*recta ratio*' (*D* 14). According to lawyers such as Coke, then, their 'artificial perfection of reason' is right reason insofar as it determines what is just and unjust, or what is legal or illegal for the King to perform (*D* 14). Certainly, it is the common law lawyers who, in Hobbes's opinion, exhibit their lack of right reason by claiming possession of it.

The political relevance of Hobbes's view of reason supports the thesis of a political influence. Since, by 1628, Hobbes was almost certainly aware of the common law lawyers' attack on the King, an attack grounded on the legalistic conception of 'right reason', there can be little doubt that this influenced Hobbes toward a contrary definition. As an aspect of natural philosophy, the definition of reason might seem 'far removed' from political concerns; in Hobbes's case, however, it is intricately related to the political problem. Given his own recognition of such relevance, it is hard to imagine that it did not influence him in some way. In addition, the thesis of a political influence provides us with an explanation for the inconsistencies in Hobbes's account of reason. As with the conventional view of truth, Hobbes has a good political reason to endorse a view of reason that denies a natural capacity for individuals to attain the truth. At the same time, however, Hobbes believes his own philosophical reasoning is right.

7.3 Summary and Possible Alternatives

I have argued that Hobbes's philosophical reasoning is influenced by his political ideas and that the recognition of such an influence provides a good explanation for some of the inconsistencies in his natural philosophy. The pattern that has emerged, I believe, provides strong evidence for an interpretation of Hobbes that takes seriously the notion of an operative political influence. We have seen, first of all, that major elements of Hobbes's natural philosophy have a direct relevance to his political ideas. Hobbes's mechanistic and materialist ontology, as Lynch points out, and Hobbes's philosophy of mind, as I have shown, may be used to undermine the politically dangerous use of Aristotelian metaphysics. Hobbes's account of dreaming may be interpreted as a direct criticism of religious prognosticators who use their dreams as evidence for their divine status. The political relevance of Hobbes's philosophy of language, insofar as it is used to combat the politically dangerous use of absurd speech, and insofar as it is important for the foundation of the commonwealth, has been pointed out by a number of scholars. Unlike other scholars, however, I have emphasized the political importance of two specific elements of Hobbes's philosophy of language, namely, his conventional view of truth and his nominalism. These two philosophical views, as we have seen, provide support for political absolutism. And finally, Hobbes's view of reason is politically relevant for its support of political absolutism and because it contests the view of reason of the common law lawyers. The presence of such a pattern, I believe, strongly suggests the existence of a political influence in Hobbes's natural philosophy. To provide further support, I will address two possible alternatives to my thesis.

7.3.a The Traditional View

It might be argued that philosophers usually have a main purpose or function in mind while composing a work. In the case of *Leviathan*, for example, it could be pointed out that Hobbes was clearly writing with the specific intention to defend his political ideas and to criticize his political opponents. Thus, the correlation between his political ideas and his natural philosophy does not need to be interpreted as evidence of a political influence. Instead, as this objection would have it, Hobbes simply used his natural philosophy as a political weapon. After having developed his natural philosophy, in other words, he began to recognize how it could be used for political purposes. The political relevance of Hobbes's natural philosophy, then, does not provide evidence for a political influence; it merely shows that Hobbes was aware of the political implications of a previously established natural philosophy.

This objection is made clearer by looking at a specific example. According to the traditional interpretation, Hobbes's conventional view of truth and his nominalism lead to or imply certain political conclusions. Hobbes first advocates nominalism and the conventional view of truth, in other words, and then draws out the political implications, as if his sole reason for adhering to these two views is philosophical. From this perspective, it could be objected against my interpretation that all I have done is to use the political 'implications' of Hobbes's philosophy of language as evidence for the existence of a political influence. It might be pointed out that Hobbes's conventional view of truth provides obvious support for his political conclusions precisely because these conclusions are derived from his natural philosophy. The traditional view, then, might claim that I have put the cart before the horse.

I would like to suggest, in response, that Hobbes's political solution encourages him to adhere to both nominalism and a conventional view of truth because of their ability to provide theoretical support for his political ideas. In contrast to the traditional view, such a suggestion is made reasonable on three counts. First, given Hobbes's early support of the King's prerogative and his analysis of the ideological causes of conflict, it seems likely that a conventional view of truth would appeal to him. Prior to Hobbes's attempt at establishing a science of politics, it is probable that he already believed that the King should be the final arbiter on political, moral and religious matters. With such a belief in mind, both nominalism and the conventional view of truth would be a natural choice. This is supported by the fact that Hobbes was interested in political matters prior to his interest in natural philosophy. According to the traditional view, Hobbes's major political conclusions drawn from his natural philosophy just happened to coincide with his prior political convictions. His natural philosophy, in other words, just happened to be great weapons for his cause.

Second, given the number of connections between Hobbes's natural philosophy and his political ideas, it is reasonable to assume that such connections are not coincidental. If it were the case that only the conventional view of truth was relevant to Hobbes's political ideas, then the traditional view might seem more plausible. Yet the connections are not limited solely to this view, but reveal a consistent pattern. As the present investigation has shown, many positions in Hobbes's natural philosophy have a direct relevance to his political ideas. Since many positions in Hobbes's natural philosophy perfectly align with his political ideas, which he possessed prior to his discovery of geometry, the traditional interpretation seems insufficient.

Third, the thesis of the political influence on Hobbes's natural philosophy provides an explanation for inconsistencies found in his views of truth, universals and reason. The traditional view, which claims Hobbes's political ideas are implications of his natural philosophy, must find ways to explain the discussed inconsistencies.

The examination of the philosophical solutions to the inconsistencies reveals that most of the solutions fall into a general type. The vast majority of Hobbes interpreters admit that his texts are inconsistent. The goal of the interpreter, however, is to find the most consistent position given the textual evidence, i.e., the one that Hobbes would agree to, assuming the inconsistency was pointed out to him. With regard to nominalism, for example, Watkins 'can see no escape from the conclusion that his statement that some names are names of accidents is inconsistent with his statement that there is nothing universal in the world but names'.[7] This inconsistency leads Watkins to claim that 'Hobbes did not subscribe to such a [conventional] view of truth because he did not abide by his radical nominalism.'[8] Although he explicitly endorses both nominalism and a conventional view of truth, Watkins implies, Hobbes does not really hold either of these positions. Hungerland and Vick provide another example of a traditional approach to resolving inconsistencies in the texts. 'What circumstances', they ask, 'are responsible for the widespread misinterpretation of Hobbes's philosophy of language by eminent scholars?'[9] In answer to this question, they provide four reasons: (1) mistakes in the English translation of *De Corpore*, (2) Hobbes's originality, (3) Hobbes's 'carelessness', (4) the failure to recognize how Hobbes's 'sketchy' philosophy of language is part of a larger system.[10] These four factors are responsible for the inconsistencies scholars normally find in Hobbes's philosophy of language. Notice that Hungerland and Vick believe they have found the most consistent reading of Hobbes, a reading that requires one to recognize Hobbes's own 'carelessness'. Although some of the blame for the inconsistencies is to be put on scholars interpreting Hobbes, Hungerland and Vick reveal that Hobbes himself is partly responsible. This is due to the fact that Hobbes's texts, in many cases, *are* blatantly inconsistent or contradictory. By correcting Hobbes's own errors, it is believed, we may arrive at the 'correct' view.

The thesis of the political influence provides us with an

explanation for the 'carelessness' that leads to inconsistencies in Hobbes; it provides us with a reason why Hobbes did not see, or did not address, glaring inconsistencies in his work. While I do not criticize the attempt at finding the most consistent position in Hobbes's works, I do point out the failure of not recognizing a political influence. Although it is possible that the inconsistencies in Hobbes's philosophy of language might simply be due to his sloppy thinking and writing, the thesis of the political influence provides a better explanation for two reasons. First, it is more charitable. It provides a reasonable excuse for Hobbes's lack of care in presenting these issues. Second, Hobbes is generally accepted as one of the great philosophers in history, precisely because of his mental acuity. To overlook such mistakes, one might argue, requires a stronger reason than simple carelessness.

7.3.b The Development of Thought View

Since Hobbes's career spanned almost 50 years, his thought clearly must have gone through a number of changes. Given this fact, one could object that the inconsistencies in Hobbes's texts result from the development of his philosophy over time. In their interpretations of Hobbes's major works, most scholars adhere to what F. S. McNeilly calls the 'consistency principle'.[11] According to this principle, Hobbes's major works are 'expressions of a single Hobbesian philosophy which did not develop or change in any important respects'.[12] McNeilly, on the other hand, claims it is virtually impossible to find consistency on any important topics:

> The upholder of the consistency principle should try to produce a single and consistent Hobbesian view on any two or three of the following topics: definitions, contingent propositions, philosophical method, truth, final causes, pleasure, desire, vital motion, glory.[13]

Unlike most scholars, McNeilly gives an in-depth analysis of the maturation of Hobbes's thought in order to explain certain inconsistencies. McNeilly's basic point is that it is important to recognize and properly deal with the fact that Hobbes's thought evolved over time. Surprisingly, this point is rarely discussed in the secondary literature.[14]

In my investigation of Hobbes's philosophy of language and of his view of reason, I used resources from different time periods. A possible objection, then, is that Hobbes's views on these matters may be more consistent than I have pointed out. This objection, however, does not have any real force since the specific inconsistencies I discussed are all found within individual texts. Inconsistent comments on the nature of truth and nominalism are found within *De Corpore*, for example. McNeilly even recognizes this fact: '[In] *De Corpore* different accounts [of truth] were given, in flat contradiction of each other.'[15] The inconsistencies in Hobbes's philosophy of language, then, are not the result of the maturation of his thought. In discussing the inconsistencies of Hobbes's view of reason, I have already addressed this point.

7.4 Conclusion

This investigation has attempted to counteract the dominant mode of interpreting the relationship between the various branches of Hobbes's philosophy. The significance of this work, however, extends beyond the scope of Hobbes scholarship and into the realm of the history of philosophy in general. With relation to Hobbes scholarship, I have contended that the nature of the political influence is systematic; that is, it thoroughly penetrates Hobbes's natural philosophy. In the history of Hobbes scholarship, only a handful of interpreters explicitly address the political influence on Hobbes's natural philosophy.[16] In cases where such influence is noted, it is done so in passing. Our understanding of Hobbes's philosophy is enhanced, I suggest, through the thesis of a political influence.

With relation to the history of philosophy in general, this work encourages an approach to the interpretation of philosophy that is overlooked by many philosophers. While debates about the social and political influences on scientific thought have been an important part of the history and philosophy of science since Thomas Kuhn published his book on the nature of scientific revolutions, many historians of philosophy have failed to take into serious consideration the operation of social and political forces on the development of philosophical thought.[17] This could be due to the fact, as David Boonin-Vail points out, that such an approach faces a serious difficulty. The 'difficulty of establishing such a claim about heuristical influences within Hobbes's thinking', Boonin-Vail says, is 'reflected in the fact that one could account for much of the same textual evidence and reach precisely the opposite conclusion'.[18] Although Boonin-Vail is correct to a certain extent, he does not mention that this problem is endemic to philosophical interpretation as a whole. In addition, as Steinberg notes, interpreters may be disinclined to consider the social and political influences on natural philosophy since doing so seems to reduce philosophy to ideology.[19] It is likely, however, that philosophers cannot ever be completely free from the effects of ideology. Nevertheless, if interpreters focus on the social and political influences on philosophical thought, which I have done in the present work, then we may be more apt to examine our own thoughts for ideological influences. Although such influences may never be eradicated, an awareness of them leads to a better understanding of our own ideas and the reasons why we hold them.

Notes

1. See Chapter 2.
2. Kavka, G. (1983), 'Right Reason and Natural Law in Hobbes's Ethics', *The Monist*, 66, 121.
3. See *L* 5.112; *L* 5.113; *L* 5.116.

4. The topic is virtually ignored in the most important works in Hobbes scholarship. It receives little or no attention in Gauthier, D. (1969), *The Logic of Leviathan*. Oxford: Clarendon Press; Hungerland, I. and Vick, G. (1981), 'Hobbes's Theory of Language, Speech, and Reasoning', in Hobbes, T., *Thomas Hobbes: Part I of De Corpore*. A. Martinich (trans.). New York: Abaris; McNeilly, F. S. (1968), *The Anatomy of Leviathan*. London: St Martin's Press; Warrender, H. (1957), *The Political Philosophy of Thomas Hobbes: His Theory of Obligation*. Oxford: Clarendon Press; Watkins, J. (1965), *Hobbes's System of Ideas*. London: Hutchinson & Co. Although Kavka devotes an article to the concept of right reason, he does not put much energy into this particular problem: see Kavka, 'Right Reason and Natural Law'.

5. See Section 3.3.b.

6. See Sections 3.1 and 3.3.c.

7. Watkins, *Hobbes's System*, p. 107.

8. Ibid.

9. Hungerland and Vick, 'Hobbes's Theory of Language, Speech, and Reasoning', p. 22.

10. Ibid., pp. 22–3.

11. McNeilly, F. S. (1993), 'Egoism in Hobbes', in Preston King (ed.), *Thomas Hobbes: Critical Assessments*. London: Routledge, Vol. 2, p. 162. First published in McNeilly, F. S. (1966), *Philosophical Quarterly*, 16, 193–206.

12. Ibid.

13. Ibid.

14. Charles Hinnant puts special emphasis on the growth of Hobbes's philosophy in Hinnant, C. (1977), *Thomas Hobbes*. Boston, MA: Twayne Publishers.

15. Ibid., p. 88.

16. In this small handful of those who explicitly address the political influence are William Lynch, Steven Shapin and Simon Shapiro. See Lynch, W. T. (1991), 'Politics in Hobbes's Mechanics: The Social as Enabling', *Studies in the History of the Philosophy of Science*, 22 (2), 295–320; Shapin, S. and Shapiro, S. (1985), *Leviathan and the Air-Pump: Hobbes, Boyle, and the Experimental Life*. Princeton, NJ: Princeton University Press.

17. Kuhn, T. (1970), *The Structure of Scientific Revolutions*. Chicago, IL: University of Chicago Press.

18. Boonin-Vail, D. (1994), *Thomas Hobbes and the Science of Moral Virtue*. Cambridge: Cambridge University Press, p. 11, fn. 24.

19. Jules, S. (1988), *The Obsession of Thomas Hobbes: The English Civil War in Hobbes's Political Philosophy*. New York: Peter Lang, pp. 2–3.

Bibliography

Aaron, R. (1967), *The Theory of Universals*. Oxford: Clarendon Press.

Adams, M. M. (1987), *William Ockham*. Notre Dame: University of Notre Dame Press.

Armstrong, D. M. (1978), *Nominalism and Realism: Universal and Scientific Realism*. Cambridge: Cambridge University Press.

Aubrey, J. (1972), *Aubrey's Brief Lives*. O. L. Dick (ed). Harmondsworth: Penguin.

Ball, T. (1981), 'Hobbes's Linguistic Turn', *Polity*, 17, 739–60.

Barnouw, J. (1989), 'Hobbes's Psychology of Thought: Endeavours, Purpose and Curiosity', *History of European Ideas*, 10, 519–45.

Berns, L. (1987), 'Thomas Hobbes', in L. Strauss and J. Cropsey (eds), *History of Political Philosophy*. Chicago, IL: University of Chicago Press.

Biletzki, A (1997), *Talking Wolves: Thomas Hobbes on the Language of Politics and the Politics of Language*. Dordrecht: Kluwer Academic Publishers.

Bloor, D. (1976), *Knowledge and Social Imagery*. London: Routledge and Kegan Paul.

Blumenberg, H. (1983), *The Legitimacy of the Modern Age*. Robert Wallace (trans.). Cambridge, MA: MIT Press.

Boonin-Vail, D. (1994), *Thomas Hobbes and the Science of Moral Virtue*. Cambridge: Cambridge University Press.

Callaghan, G. K. (2001), 'Nominalism, Abstraction, and Generality in Hobbes', *History of Philosophy Quarterly*, 18, 41.

Cantalupo, C. (1991), *A Literary Leviathan: Thomas Hobbes's Masterpiece of Language*. Lewisburg, PA: Bucknell University Press.

Courtenay, W. (1990), *Capacity and Volition: A History of the Distinction of Absolute and Ordained Power*. Bergamo: Pierluigi Lubrina.

de Crespigny, A. and Minogue, K. (1975), 'Introduction', in A. de Crespigny and K. Minogue (eds), *Contemporary Political Philosophy*. New York: Mead and Company.

Curley, E. (1994), 'Introduction to Hobbes's *Leviathan*', in E. Curley (ed.), *Leviathan*. Indianapolis, IN: Hackett Publishing.

Danford, J. (1980), 'The Problem of Language in Hobbes's Political Science', *Journal of Politics*, 42, 102–34.

Descartes, R. (1984), *The Philosophical Writings of Descartes*. 2 Vols. J. Cottingham, R. Stoothoff and D. Murdoch (trans.). Cambridge: Cambridge University Press.

Ewin, R. E. (1991), *Virtue and Rights: The Moral Philosophy of Thomas Hobbes*. San Francisco, CA: Westview Press.

Field, H. (1980), *Science without Numbers: A Defense of Nominalism*. Princeton, NJ: Princeton University Press.

Finn, S. (2002), 'Geometry and the Science of Morality in Hobbes', in C. Hughes and J. Wong (eds), *Communication, Conflict, and Reconciliation: Social Philosophy Today*. Charlottesville, VA: Philosophy Documentation Center .

Gauthier, D. (1969), *The Logic of Leviathan: The Moral and Political Theory of Thomas Hobbes*. Oxford: Clarendon Press.

Gert, B. (1965a), 'Hobbes and Psychological Egoism', *Journal of the History of Ideas*, 28, 503–20.

— (1965b), 'Hobbes, Mechanism, and Egoism', *Philosophical Quarterly*, 15, 341–9.

Goldsmith, M. M. (1966), *Hobbes's Science of Politics*. New York: Columbia University Press.

Hampton, J. (1986), *Hobbes and the Social Contract Tradition*. Cambridge: Cambridge University Press.

Hansen, D. (1990), 'The Meaning of "Demonstration" in Hobbes's Science', *History of Political Thought*, 11, 587–626.

Herbert, G. (1989), *Thomas Hobbes: The Unity of Scientific and Moral Wisdom*. Vancouver: University of British Columbia Press.

Hinnant, C. (1977), *Thomas Hobbes*. Boston, MA: Twayne Publishers.

Hobbes, T. (1841a), *An Answer to Bishop Bramhall*, in W. Molesworth (ed.), *The English Works of Thomas Hobbes of Malmesbury*. London: John Bohn, Vol. 4.

— (1969), 'A Short Tract on First Principles', in F. Toennies (ed.), *Elements of Law*. London: Frank Cass and Company Limited.

— (1841b), *Behemoth*, in W. Molesworth (ed.), *The English Works of Thomas Hobbes of Malmesbury*. London: John Bohn, Vol. 6.

— (1841c), *Considerations upon the Reputation of Thomas Hobbes*, in W. Molesworth (ed.), *The English Works of Thomas Hobbes of Malmesbury*. London: John Bohn, Vol. 6.

— (1991), *De Cive*, in B. Gert (ed.), *Thomas Hobbes: Man and Citizen*. Indianapolis, IN: Hackett Publishing.

— (1841d), *De Corpore*, in W. Molesworth (ed.), *The English Works of Thomas Hobbes of Malmesbury*. London: John Bohn, Vol. 1.

— (1972), *De Homine*, in B. Gert (ed.), *Man and Citizen*. Charles T. Wood, T. S. K. Scott-Craig and Bernard Gert (trans.). Garden City, NY: Doubleday.

— (1841e), *A Dialogue between a Philosopher and a Student of the Common Laws of England*, in W. Molesworth (ed.), *The English Works of Thomas Hobbes of Malmesbury*. London: John Bohn, Vol. 6.

— (1841f), *Eight Books of the Peloponnesian War written by Thucydides the Son of Olorus, interpreted with Faith and Diligence immediately out of the Greek by Thomas Hobbes*, in W. Molesworth (ed.), *The English Works of Thomas Hobbes of Malmesbury*. London: John Bohn, Vols. 8–9.

— (1969), *Elements of Law*. F. Toennies (ed.). London: Frank Cass and Company Limited.

— (1985) *Leviathan*. C. B. Macpherson (ed). London: Penguin Classics.

— (1841g), *On Liberty and Necessity*, in W. Molesworth (ed.), *The English Works of Thomas Hobbes of Malmesbury*. London: John Bohn, Vol. 4.

— (1727), *Principia et Problemata aliquot Geometricia*, In V. Mandey (ed.), *Mellificium Mensionis; or, the Marrow of Measuring*. V. Mandey (trans.). London: Tho. Tebb and others.

— (1841h), *Six Lessons to the Savilian Professors of the Mathematics*, in W. Molesworth (ed.), *The English Works of Thomas Hobbes of Malmesbury*. London: John Bohn, Vol. 7.

— (1839), *Thomas Hobbes Malmesburiensis opera philosophica quae latine scripsit omnia*. W. Molesworth (ed.). London: John Bohn, Vol. 1.

Hughes, A. (1991), *The Causes of the English Civil War*. New York: St Martin's Press.

Hungerland, I. and Vick, G. (1981), 'Hobbes's Theory of Language, Speech, and Reasoning', in Hobbes, T., *Thomas Hobbes: Part I of De Corpore*. A. Martinich (trans.). New York: Abaris.

Johnson, C. (1985), 'The Hobbesian Conception of Sovereignty and Aristotle's Politics', *Journal of the History of Ideas*, 46, 327–47.

Johnston, D. (1986), *The Rhetoric of Leviathan: Thomas Hobbes and the Politics of Cultural Transformation*. Princeton, NJ: Princeton University Press.

de Jong, W. (1990), 'Did Hobbes Have a Semantic Theory of Truth?', *Journal of the History of Philosophy*, 28, 63–88.

Jules, S. (1988), *The Obsession of Thomas Hobbes: The English Civil War in Hobbes's Political Philosophy*. New York: Peter Long.

Karskens, M. (1982), 'Hobbes's Mechanistic Theory of Science, and its Role in his Anthropology', in J. G. van der Bend (ed.), *Thomas Hobbes: His View of Man*. Amsterdam: Rodopi B.V.

Kavka, G. (1986), *Hobbesian Moral and Political Theory*. Princeton, NJ: Princeton University Press.

— (1983), 'Right Reason and Natural Law in Hobbes's Ethics', *The Monist*, 66, 120–33.

Kraynack, R. P. (1990), *History and Modernity in the Thought of Thomas Hobbes*. Ithaca, NY: Cornell University Press.

Kuhn, T. (1970), *The Structure of Scientific Revolution*. Chicago, IL: University of Chicago Press.

Laird, J. (1943), 'Hobbes on Aristotle's *Politics*', *Proceedings of the Aristotelian Society*, 43, 1–20.

Laudan, L. (1977), *Progress and Its Problems*. Berkeley, CA: University of California Press.

Leff, G. (1976), *The Dissolution of the Medieval Outlook: An Essay on Intellectual and Spiritual Change in the Fourteenth Century*. New York: New York University Press.

Leshen, J. (1985), 'Reason and Perception in Hobbes: An Inconsistency', *Nous*, 19, 429–37.

Lloyd, S. A. (1992), *Ideals as Interests in Hobbes's Leviathan: The Power of Mind over Matter*. Cambridge: Cambridge University Press.

Lott, T. (1982), 'Hobbes's Mechanistic Psychology', in J. G. van der Band (ed.), *Thomas Hobbes: His View of Man*. Amsterdam: Rodopi B.V.

— (1974), 'Motivation and Egoism in Hobbes', *Kinesis*, 6, 112–25.

Lynch, W. T. (1991), 'Politics in Hobbes's Mechanics: The Social as Enabling', *Studies in the History of the Philosophy of Science*, 22 (2), 295–320.

Macpherson, C. B. (1968), 'Introduction to *Leviathan*', in Hobbes, T., *Leviathan*. C. B. Macpherson (ed.). Harmondsworth: Penguin.

— (1962), *Political Theory of Possessive Individualism*. Oxford: Oxford University Press.

Martinich, A. P. (1999), *Hobbes: A Biography*. Cambridge: Cambridge University Press.

— (1992), *The Two Gods of Leviathan*. Cambridge: Cambridge University Press.

Mathie, W. (1986), 'Reason and Rhetoric in Hobbes's *Leviathan*', *Interpretation*, 14, 281–98.

McMullin, E. (1984), 'The Rational and the Social in the History of Science', in J. R. Brown (ed.), *Scientific Rationality: The Sociological Turn*. Dordrecht: D. Riedel Publishing Company.

McNeilly, F. S. (1968), *The Anatomy of Leviathan*. London: St Martin's Press.

— (1993), 'Egoism in Hobbes', in Preston King (ed.), *Thomas Hobbes: Critical Assessments*. London: Routledge, Vol. 2, p. 162. First published in McNeilly, F. S. (1966), *Philosophical Quarterly*, 16, 193–206.

Molesworth, W. (ed.), *The English Works of Thomas Hobbes of Malmesbury*. London: John Bohn.

Nerney, G. (1985), 'Hobbes: The Twofold Grounding of Civil Philosophy', *History of Philosophy Quarterly*, 2 (4), 395–409.

Oakeshott, M. (1962), *Hobbes on Civil Association*. New York: Cromwell-Collier.

Peters, R. (1956), *Hobbes*. Harmondsworth: Penguin Books.

Plamenatz, J. P. (1963) *Man and Society: Political and Social Theory: Machiavelli through Rousseau*. Vol. 1. New York: McGraw-Hill Book Company.

Plato (1981), *Five Dialogues*. G. M. A. Grube (trans.). Indianapolis, IN: Hackett Publishing.

Reik, M. (1977), *The Golden Lands of Thomas Hobbes*. Detroit, MI: Wayne State University Press.

Riedel, M. (1982), 'Paradigm Evolution in Political Philosophy: Aristotle and Hobbes', *Graduate Faculty Philosophy Journal*, 9, 109–23.

Rogow, A. A. (1986), *Thomas Hobbes: Radical in the Service of Reaction*. New York: W. W. Norton & Company.

Ross, G. M. (1988), 'Hobbes and Descartes on the Relation between Language and Consciousness', *Synthese*, 75, 217–29.

Russell, C. (1979), *Parliaments and English Politics 1621–1629*. Oxford: Clarendon Press.

Russell, R. (1939), *Natural Law in the Philosophy of Thomas Hobbes*. Dissertation for the Doctorate in the Faculty of Philosophy of the Pontifical Gregorian University.

Sacksteder, W. (1980), 'Hobbes: The Art of Geometricians', *Journal of the History of Philosophy*, 18, 131–46.

— (1979), 'Speaking About Mind: *Endeavour* in Hobbes', *The Philosophical Forum*, 11, 65–79.

— (1992), 'Three Diverse Sciences in Hobbes: First Philosophy, Geometry, and Physics', *Review of Metaphysics*, 45, 739–72.

Sarasohn, L. T. (1985), 'Motion and Morality: Pierre Gassendi, Thomas Hobbes, and the Mechanical World-View', *Journal of the History of Ideas*, 46, 363–79.

Sepper, D. (1988), 'Imagination, Phantasms, and the Making of Hobbesian and Cartesian Science', *Monist*, 71, 526–42.

Shapin, S. and Shapiro, S. (1985), *Leviathan and the Air-Pump: Hobbes, Boyle, and the Experimental Life*. Princeton, NJ: Princeton University Press.

Shelton, G. (1992), *Morality and Sovereignty in the Philosophy of Hobbes*. New York: St Martin's Press.

Skinner, Q. (1996), *Reason and Rhetoric in the Philosophy of Hobbes*. Cambridge: Cambridge University Press.

Soles, D. H. (1996), *Strong Wits and Spider Webs: A Study in Hobbes's Philosophy of Language*. Aldershot: Ashgate Publishing.

Sommerville, J. P. (1992), *Thomas Hobbes: Political Ideas in Historical Context*. London: MacMillan.

Sorell, T. (1988), 'Descartes, Hobbes and the Body of Natural Science', *Monist*, 71, 515–25.

— (1986), *Hobbes*. London: Routledge and Kegan Paul.

Spragens, T. (1973), *The Politics of Motion: The World of Thomas Hobbes: Its Basis and Genesis*. Lexington, KY: University of Kentucky Press.

Steinberg, J. (1988), *The Obsession of Thomas Hobbes: The English Civil War in Hobbes's Political Philosophy*. New York: Peter Lang.

Strauss, L. (1952), *The Political Philosophy of Hobbes: Its Basis and Genesis*. Chicago, IL: University of Chicago Press.

Talaska, R. (1988), 'Analytic and Synthetic Method According to Hobbes', *Journal of the History of Philosophy*, 26, 207–37.

Tuck, R. (1988), 'Hobbes and Descartes', in G. A. J. Rogers and A. Ryan (eds), *Perspectives on Thomas Hobbes*. Oxford: Clarendon Press.

Verdon, M. (1982), 'On the Laws of Physical and Human Nature: Hobbes's Physical and Social Cosmologies', *Journal of the History of Ideas*, 43, 653–63.

Warrender, H. (1957), *The Political Philosophy of Thomas Hobbes: His Theory of Obligation*. Oxford: Clarendon Press.

Watkins, J. (1965), *Hobbes's System of Ideas*. London: Hutchinson & Co.

Whelan, F. (1981), 'Language and Its Abuses in Hobbes's Political Philosophy', *American Political Science Review*, 75, 59–75.

Index